Wormwood Vermouth,
Warphistory

For Marilyn
with love,
Charles

righting the photon
              or the arch 'to err'

the kick of idiom

Wormwood Vermouth,
Warphistory

Charles Noble

Thistledown Press Ltd.

© 1995, Charles Noble
All rights reserved

Canadian Cataloguing in Publication Data
Noble, Charles, 1945 -

Wormwood, vermouth, warphistory

Poems.
ISBN 1-895449-36-7
I. Title.

PS8577.O32W6 1995   C811'.54   C95-920160-2
PR9199.3.N63W6 1995

Book design by A.M. Forrie
Cover art by J. Forrie
Set in Transitional 521
by Thistledown Press

Printed and bound in Canada
by Hignell Printing
Winnipeg, Manitoba

Thistledown Press Ltd.
633 Main Street
Saskatoon, Saskatchewan
S7H 0J8

An earlier version of "Guilded Writers" appeared in the twenty-first anniversary issue of *Whetstone*.

This book has been published with the assistance of The Canada Council and the Saskatchewan Arts Board

Acknowledgements:

I would like to thank Seán Virgo for his thoughtfulness, encouragement, and his "running commentary".

The author also wishes to thank the Alberta Foundation for the Arts for financial assistance in the writing of this book.

WHYTESEND WARPHISTORY IN THE NOISE LIES

to the memory of Jon Whyte

        ungava in-joke,
                wild willed
                voice, just
                "knock knock"
                the latest

                he will say
                      what you will
                      want
                      of
                      the world wave jam
     secession
* as seekwan is noise again . . .
                Echimamish . . . Etomami
       . . . hence we converse*
Inuit ungava   inwit/Whytein/no noise

                behind clouds moon
                          shines
            snow peak
                      picks out
        a sending
                up the valley

* silence is born of the marriage
        of deep wonder and winter*

GUILDED WRITERS

You don't like this title
— liken it to your likin'? —

even as aspersive lichen
participaint, in part an alga of being,
outpart a fungus

long side the *Summa Theologica* in a teaspoon
on the Thomist shore
before the vaster — even Tom Thomson lack

but like [J.O.] Thompson's "Gates of Even" —
open?

I don't like flying by instruments either, or the welding hell-
met abyss before the leap of retrospective light.

I used to think of titles as com-prehensile,
quintessentially poetic both/and deterministic.
Too so, out of hand pans the encounter-
pointbush. I can't even

remember the line now
embedded in a personal history,
intertwined with another, woman.

Rich in its spareness, in its fielding
very sarcastic, cutting

but not cutting off, actually a fight started
without her, extrapolated, brought up to date.

Washing my hands literally, bent over the sink
who could get the inside joke,
well besides you know?

Do they write novels over this sort of
oh sorry didn't know the mike was on.

He said the reason my book wasn't/on the shelf
was cuz they were doing inventory, then the next time
he said it was there so I went down to see
but it wasn't. He said then not in the poetry section
but in the chapbook section, so I looked there
and there it wasn't.

I felt quite forward and fast backward too
bringing it up again when we were on air
discussing the here here, coming electronic era.

Then when I'd given up I walked in one day
and before I could say anything his assistant said
if they're not on the shelf they're sold.
Sure, with mind-reading like this
who needs a bookstore!

And driving across the city onto memorial drive, lower case
'm', "lower casket" on the page now in a terrible
curve of retrieval, I listened to
another bookstore manager, who was not
a TV personality at all and who hosted launchings,
debate on the radio his decision to carry *Final Exit*.

In Red Deer at the Special General Meeting Reg read cold
Jon's telegram in which Jon condemned
the whole idea of the meeting.
He was going ahead with Italy
according to decisions before his diagnosis.

After my reading while Cecelia was reading
I ate an egg sandwich back in the service hallway,
all cement and pipes, and the host hunkered down
with a cigarette. I would never do that to my knees
even though I do squats once a week, deep knee bends
every morning. He asked me about various Calgary
writers and Bert Almon from Edmonton,
the chocolate bar dispelling hypothermia.

I knew Sid with his Beethoven brow
and his hypothermia blues tune too I teased.

Stole that from the Spinoza expert, Stuart Hampshire,
who used it as an argument against Wittgenstein,
ie Ludwig's idea of debate was lowering his stormy brow.
Pass the wig!

In Edmonton I read last and Cecelia said
she got a much better purchase on my poem
even tho in Calgary she hadn't/ left the room
while I read, first. How *do* you have Virginia room
left, writing, O negatively ululating wit?

When it was over people cleaned up quickly
and just about everyone was gone when I realized
I had no place to stay and no money to spare.

Oh yeah, Bert, ruminating on tabloid appeal
during his reading, said that people needed something
to believe in. "I really believe that" he said.

In Calgary he worried he'd insulted me with his poem
having some fun with a philosophy professor.
"No, he was no professor of mine" I said.

Before, he had studied the philosophy section behind me
while I talked to Robert, showing good will I surmised
since the blurb on the back of my book
said I read philosophy in the winter. It was February.

It occurs to me now, not just from a recent reference
in one of his new poems since to Aristotle
and a too-easily-taken-for-the-author's poem's swipe
at philosophy in another poem, that my speculation
on his browsing says more about me and at that
not much, a superficial narcissism!

When I straighten up from the sink I see the storm
on my brow gradually subside.

Robert is more nervous than his voice/ lets on.
You see it in his actions. When I was talking to Bert
RoBert grabbed a handful of peanuts to toss off
into his mouth like Ravens
from the elusive origin to the backwards Big Crunch.
But a Poe tic happened and Hitchcocks stormed his forehead.

Half a peanut rested lightly on his overcoat collar
as he waltzed off. I put my hand up to my mouth
to heighten the laughter not to stifle it, backed
against Heidegger's big volumes on Nietzsche,
good luck to the eyes in the back of my head.

In Edmonton Neff and I walked down Jasper Avenue
to a small, mostly empty bar and had quite a few pints.
(Sounds more like a pub, with its antique tables too.)
I was a very blocked conversationalist because I was
still at the library where the reading was now
developing its hidden personalities.

Doug Barbour and Blodgett talking we passed in the stairwell
to the underground parkade, only way out,
on whose one way ramps to the light and roar of traffic
our backward feet held cap-i'-hand full
for a car'less spell. Neff was giving me
some of the reactions around him at the reading
which made me / dumber in the bar
as it made me / library smart.

In Red Deer I mentioned all the copies of my book
were sent back to the publisher
a week after I'd had my mind read in the mystery bookstore
in the mystery city
even tho they'd all been sold — but as mysteries!

An unnamed executive member offered that she knew
the bookstore owner very well,
and through hunkered in-formed smoke I stalked the double
crossing overhead.

Two networks of power intersect, well intimations
of power, always dead intimate and no where to go.

Can you pull rancour the way here the precognition
of a pun thereupon overcomes you?

Now I think of Thompson's letter-poem from London, UK
I read to the WGA at the AGM. The obituaries, eulogies
and letter with more details I sent him
unlocked his grief over Jon. He played with the misspelling
in the Crag of "the Doges' Palace". In the spirit of Jon
he took 'Dojeys' out into blue jays, instead of pigeons,
to St. Mark's Square. "Blue jays and lions" he wrote
four times at the end. Release, refrain, a spell
on the brow, a spill in the field, the field.

'Charles, if I ask what Jon made of
"the Dojeys Palace in Venice"
as reported in the Crag and Canyon
of the high point of the Italy trip
he went ahead with while dying

it is because we both know he couldn't have
failed to make something out of such a twist.'

The rhyme of 'dying' into 'Canyon'. And when I paused
for the poetics after "he couldn't have" and again
after "failed", my voice went on me
with an exacted-by-a-hair cross purpose, hit directly by,
indirectly triggering the no-jam jamb echo shadow-flood
of irrepressible Jon.

We sat in Georgio's in Banff over pasta when he knew
his time was short, him arguing the difference
between internationalism and cosmopolitanism
as it applied to the school "up on the hill",
urging me to apply for a grant (two grants)
he would recommend me for but "get back to the lyric"
and "not for a book of essays!"

Up against the "philosophers" he put the natural scientists
any day. The depth of time they opened up
in the 19th century and now. "The Good of Pessimism
doubles — *for good measure*", my one essay
he heard read in Panorama
just before the results of his biopsy,
he kept digging me about, its grand historical tone.
And when I showed the right amount of defensiveness
he laughed and said aside "just a tonyism" and admitted
the lure of grandeur to himself, ie he was open about
what drew him. The admission was there for each of us,
shit detectors drawing our own flak.

He gives me the last word, only he is taken for it.
At his word every generate shade of meaning could be
pure Jon.   Rich
rushes, memories-as-us, as in "the rest of — "

In others we die, and live — the gross irony, both ways
asymmetric, is the twist symptom of a Nietzsche net
or old duality floated, written off into the set
it haunts and sets off.

She made us into peacocks determined as we were,
don't blame me I'm too cool. Jon's wit went supernova.
Jug, jug to ear/th (my cyclic pun) asking
"how much wine have you had?"

This conflated party — there is Jon on all fours playing
to the dog, barking at the ceiling "roof! roof!"
Then the rub on the rug, "rough! rough!" he remonstrated
and demonstrated, a "bourn", a "bodkin", a trans-mutt,
perchance to concretize.

I had been reading *Inward Bound* by Abraham Pais
that very afternoon
so asked Jon, "who discovered the electron?"

"Rutherford, 1910" he owled with glasses down his nose
already an answer observing my question.

"Whoo?!" I asked archly under everybody's audible awe
but too drunk myself and laughing
to have out with my quickly decaying physics
the correct "J.J. Thompson, 1897."

After the opening events Friday night at Panorama
some of us stayed up late and drank, listened to Jon
carefully unfold some set piece stories. He betrayed
nothing beyond the story at hand but drank only pop
and quit the cigarettes. I interrupted the China shop
to correct his grammar, Jon on Jon, case of plural noun,
singular verb. He paused, pursed his lips as I weakly
thought out out loud "oh yeah you're right, plural noun
quoted as word." A forgotten word, attracts me strangely
terribly now, the way retracing which loses a link
flowers into miraculous birth, within which fit-to-be-
tied one would undo back, unearth an old shoe or kernel
the grain of which skin, like an underclass, would call up
more than would call down any set-to all set above all
not to remember being mixed-up in the weak infinite
frictions — to leave the stateless, milled white aura-gone
dust, the total trust of conditional half lives uncalled-for
re-quantized into *his* wild "omniscient" whoop — warp hear.

He'd have remembered too or we'd have bantered
into a reconstruction. He the archivist of a choice ark
always splitting into re-portaging canoe heads.
"Don't Noah any better" I could say in his spirit, again,
here figuring substance through the kick of idiom.

A *Year In Provence* was what I thought he wanted
read in December in the hospital " . . . against . . . sempiternal
ahness . . . protracted comedy, which glitters against
the darkness", the ho ho, but with warmer light
than exceptional Lewis tested double blind.

I read for twenty minutes and paused to look
at his closed lids. "I'm listening" he said
and a few minutes later corrected my French.

The last time I saw him I looked — like a cliché
around the door and met his slightly bugging eyes
slightly watered, not otherworldly but "the melancholy
inherent in the animal life." He signaled me to his "this" side
for hearing best, bugged by the begged body raised
to overshadow anything we could add
and did a kind of elbow sit up. "I can still do this."
When I touched his shoulder he "jumped".
"You have a Happy Christmas" I said unreally
before I left, pathetic and pathetic.

Ironic Grinch with an interfering kindliness
he stole my name by degrees into anybody's
interactive adjective between lives, cut a figure
in his middle brow, undercut me with a quick
"Happy Christmas" back, like his mock 60's
"flame within the flame" without
the "mock".

SQUARE ROOT OF HIP

I would just like to sit down, have a cup of coffee,
say java without a hitch

and not think about
how good it feels.

I think not, Java man

thinking is the biggest thing.

I feel is therefore the all important missing link,
burns you in effigy.

I feel is the chemistry with fingerprints
in case your predicates fly off your predicaments.

A dictator lives,
won't die

goes retro, even religious, or dictionary
in the sense of extra-uterine, walking dictionaries — pocket
outlaws, hip and stir crazy precluding and re-presenting
time as surplus spellings-out, misfit for itself,
skeletalizing the present into the closet, secret passages.
Every conversation opens into this shock
of the friendly aliens, into this antechamber of commerce
in the dark and dies
into a role model. Down the road you
change a tire, a wheel nut rolls into the gravel,
another indistinguishable die. When you find it
diamond facets don't flash but flesh out the engineer's dream,
a bolt of miniaturized lightning turns the chemistry upset
into life as we know it, quasi time's wrenching puns
with and without words.

I would just like to sit down coffee, do I take cream?
I don't cry my guts out, I eat with them, they eat away,

I listen to entrails happy little killings
at the false nerve ending.

The northern lights are asbestos green as best as I can tell
but red behind the garage.

I stand in the dark yard, head back, drop-jawed,
body waffle and wax while my strained face
relaxes. Re piss hard-ons, already literary
(death goes better with God free),
I think to check Freud on dream flying,
intra-uterine swimming memory too: *will*
with a mind of its own.

Your sex life has nine lives and always ends futile up on top
Thank-you, fog , but is not so much points/mass carnal
as reincarnal possessed, it is the wealth of nations
that can't park its wilderness in its second nature
and so drives the economy, ie your 19th century sex life.
Or look homeward angel, Canada interpellated.
It thought it would just die!

But the nation state is needed to baffle the undamned
rising tide who deliver themselves the currency
that alternates to the threat of "equal" and opposite
withdrawals, the potent soul of the difference machines
making for the actual, derivative withdrawals — the instant
adjustment in the balance, and the desire*able* slight
delay in the loss of symptoms of the loss-of phase.

History-scrapers collapse, scarfolds of language remain
stuck in the collective craw spaces.

The bladder works in mysterious ways, the body chip
has a mental block, economy is not just to piss through,
to piss away your sex life, to die, the old winged pun,
and remain living without wings or the *Melody of Theology*
or even the Peircean melody of thirdness.
Firstness as far as possible.

My mother's arthritic aunt said
she washed from the top down as far as possible
and from the bottom up as far as possible.

Asked my grandfather, Labour Legislature wit,
"what about her possible?"

— my possible grandfather and mother's aunt, relieved
from the farce of firstness by the melody of thirdness
recoiled from the noise, or the *it moved* — one shard of sky,
one "aching" strut of pure confusion, pre-stressed,
pre-constructed history — uncovered

to reliving back a touching march in nested burlesque,
an empty re-sounding ache — the *it moves me still* strut
of history covered.

Waiting for a call back, stomach begins wringing its hands.
Food massage is the message and an overdetermined variety
of infections knot up, something not coming down.

Under the cushion on the couch I found a caramel.
I thanked her in the morning for the use of her couch
and the camel's dry spell, rolling my 'r's I tossed and turned
and thanked her dramatically, hanging from the monkey bars
of my stage presence, counting back into the still wrapped
caramel I shat neat like an Easter bunny
from the square root of hip.

Got scolded by Anne Szumigalski through a second party
through the mail on the correct tenses of 'shit'.
A vowel movement tweaks an aura into powder.

Between 'shit' and 'shat' is a tense position.
"Shit" via *aufheben* is literary effort,
as in yesterday's "man", extruding literature out of itself,
ie laying out red carpet for visiting life.

'Shat' is a sad stink
through a cellophane darkly.

The Garneau theatre is open again.
Twenty-eight years ago I saw Elvis at a sneak preview
in a movie within a movie. The surrounding movie was worse
than the movie within and further, three drunken engineers
sat behind me, girlfriend-acted upon, complex modifier,
vector analysis too much. Will I ever see the internal damage?

Invariant in a vacuum
the Ernst Bloch of hope has no rest mass.
Friction for the arrow of time but the gravel
rolls me back, Camus appearance
pushing into a rising "world line"of dashed hope,
can't see over the hedge, *The Shining*.

Imagination down, almost living in buzzed-up empiricism,
lost all my adolescent clones, shell game. I *was* there,
quicker than beheld I have to hand it to the future
a great privilege exposed to a birth, a general relativity
crowding-out effect, "the ubiquity of the normative"
righting the photon.

Brain mobilized, measured out in coffee stanzas,
brittle with going for it, nervous about today's balance sheet.
I like something about "balance sheet", hate something
about its type, figuratives not adding up.

'Pee' I hate, sexier than 'piddle' I always thought had 't's.
'Piss' errs on the other side but right on urethra,
K. Burke's demon anger rooted, at least analogically.
A phoneme and an emotion like the sword and snakes
twist, not my words, but my psychosomatic attitude.

Body goes around for your flat-out fulfillment
and your flattened hopes, reduces your missing links
to worry juice, ends in bad breath elephants I say

Solomonly, half child missing and picture thinking up
nowhere between *eloquent* and *elegance*.

Ends in bad breath the confession of an anchorite going back
to the well, Rousseau-moored amour untying the tongue.
Pound of swelled head re-entered to foot medallions.

I look at the sky fade, the lit-up, rich red bar
above the driver that says "bathroom occupied".

The soundless TVs carry *The Hunt for Red October*,
unretorting gas gives me the inwit to inspissate,
one of Bertrand Russell's ten favourite words which are
dislocated, hip for him and hymnal in an ether orth/au —
monotheistically distilled into the law of the universe/
returned scientifically to the polymorphous reverse.
The sky in patches and vague bars is incarnadine,

another of his ten favourites. All I have to say now
is: alembic

for the Hannah Arendt-ed love of the world
in a word, out / living
a big mammal's in-stance, longer like a species than the big
terminal cathedrals — graven tokens flown not flowing
from the benedictionary
in turn spirited away from any benefactor.

Which *comes* first of word and world
opens a different ontology from which *came* first
even if the answers are the same.

But I have the urge to say
"alembic pentameter".

I still have a trace liking for the word 'expedite'
though my mind typically especially goes crossword blank
with this Latin readymade as I walk to the light switch
while my body count has an out of mind experience.

You hand your fake ID to the liquor store clerk
before pictures were the bright idea.

He quizzes you and you blow your birthday,
go flame-decaled with old genies, bottled-up girlfriends.

You were twenty-one anyway without any idea
so took the false one just in case of some surplus
you had to start killing in that mysterious sense of 'it'
that disappears but you feel the effects of
released into the mother of all sameness,
squares of departure.

Someone squirts wine at you from a wine skin.
Your conversation at first can't seem to find your mouth.

Oliver stones Jim Morrison right back to an archetype
"tempted to exist" "out of here alive". *The Rite of Spring*
on the cusp — where's the meta-question to insure
the currency of life and while it's at it, the usage values
of 'currency'? Is it better — meta blank word rubber checking
but digging for — the hole of the messiah handle — is it better
to angle in the expense of spirit full blown and thus come
to angel any way
is a trip
wiring you up for nerves, drowning in *drowning out*,
white robe and eternally mint on the mossy bank, or — I've lost
my oar, let alone my ruddy rood.

History not squaring with the historian's cap-
tive subject-
ivity
after a long day's narrativ-
ity, Frank Zap-Pa, radical square, not the type
to die young, always the old kidder, much beater, off, alive
to hip's latest earlier, lights a wicked cubist wick
over the Doors' "the end" and this, the other end
baby or candle-handled *Firebird*.

Wild camping in the compound
matrix. Rocky aura show

Blue Velvet hangs in the night, with a zap absorbs
the bugged-out dark. (What's bugging America, Hardy Boys?
Bugs are real [at first I thought the cut-off ear
was a used condom]. The two Blacks are required
in the hardware because one is blind
but like *The Shining* lumbering through the movie
he geist right how many fingers
and then the axe is handed over/ the counter
so they can read the price tag on the head
and get split in two. America is bugs. Ambiguous America
is buggered up. Dennis Hopper is a real bugger,
a long way from the nice young, miscegenetic doctor in *Giant*.
The Hardy boy hides in the closet, a human, Kafka bug —
easy riding Hopper gives cockroach a funny second life,
the roach (cock) down to nothing he violently sucks pure —
oxygen is it? — bugging, apart from the obligatory
electronics, the room. His cover is as fumigator, de-bugger
allegory chasing allegory, willing into the well,
down the sick well.)

US dissidents are select Canadians to a fault.
With so much negative Canadian space we can afford to be
"Americans" being Canadian by default. Beavers lodging
complaints under water and up into little Canadas
pock-marking moon-strapped *Amerika* these *Ancient Evenings*
getting older in the gravid, disincarnating dust-up.
Chomsky the big operates from base Canada
(both soil and somewhere
Eli-ing in the generated "life sentences" which exceed
the country of origin/ seed the cloud of its sublime
accomodation)

which necessarily openly bugs with high mind the high hand —
*o holy ghost dip your finger in the blood of Canada and write,
I love you* (Margaret comes out of the Atwood
dives into the deep anti
apart from any Shields [Canadian Carol or otherwise]
to where the gene is open in the genie's surfacing

at wood — rough-cut genus as buried axiom,
fin de pieces of any scale like teeth square
in the raw root —

turns herself into herself
with a birthing beaver lodgic,
twigs to the cracking of the combi-nation
country of underground procedures
for the unlimited other within the limited, "Ricoeuring" self.)

(Black Rose Press, Massey Lectures, *Briarpatch*, all Rick
Salutin Noam — pace Brian-running-hot-and-cold-good-cop-
bad-cop-picking-up-the-bracketing-zeroing-in-pace [nay to
19th century Alice Munro and nay to 21st century "language
poets"]-can-he-keep-up-the-pace Fawcett.)

Who's left in the brackets? Brian!, the old "performing self"
"majority of one". But even Brian keeps
his holding company of authorities, like everybody's baby
(and see *Moscow Diary* of a hapless child, without
confusing it with Arendt's biographical sketch and his event-
ual, flush-with-history death), Walter Benjamin
Leo Bersani demon?strates finally to be no "fine-tuned,
unsentimental Marxist [aesthetic method-ist]"
but confused messianic anti-historian, and finally, final cult
-worshipper, ie like *worship*-worshipper is his history
"blasting". Exactly, true to his hero, global McLuhan,
what is to Brian to be hated! Nasty invectives —
stinking cults and kabals! And he even Ezra Pounds his chest
a bit here, righteously and sub-latedly.

The twentieth century work of art
should not merely "resemble a community"
as in the pusillanimous language guys but should promise
you a "model", (giving him the benefit of the Lyotarded
Kantian verb), or should float a categorical imperative?
— against, you geist it, universal chicken! I hear two hands
clapping backwards till the fish gets small again

and the agile brackets move on. Hang in there Brian.
I mean it. And me, "one of the more reneging writers"?

— the ghost in the pun Bruce F. encountered me with
because puns are three-way "out of time" waiting,
are word-nebulous — as in "rosy-fingered" say — concepts
which in turn are the limiting of words given —
to the unlimited. Puns smack of the unicorny
"synthetic a priori" as they milk their way into the night
"when all cows are black".
A figurative wave lifts off into crème de la crème
efficient meaning. Land! You promised land.
'Land' is a restoration here, meaning an aim, aiming
a meaning, tomorrow the world.

The joke question is ghost right
as I "sum over histories" correctly,
ie unavoidably between my gyroscope ears,
foolproof, restored-from-story, stupid consciousness
sub-ing for itself by constant instant, total subtraction.
Correcting the course, forever, as 'forever' twin spins
'for good' into its untemporal virtuality which intends time
back like an IAAC, kayak balance, satyr-like
in the extensions of the nervous [financial] system,
run aground in the funding environments
lending a bit of culture from the high pressure area
while the weather lasts or starts over.
Bless the hit-and-miss-back-to-square-one
live mind Fawcett re a Purdy poem. "You don't like that idea?
I've got twenty more!"

Stats Canada working the American pie out into
more decimals as way-in innumerate Johnny (bending the iron
one) Wayne meets of-Ruben-and-the-Jets Frank Zap-
pa-ta-physical (not *really big shoester*), the shyster/rube
rebel with a simple cause cele-bray of
hic jacet lepus, the hick
up to the graceless attic and puppeteer malapropped heaven

up à la Lionel Kearns a notch practising
string theory, bruiting and fingering up
the loop holes in the loop holes in the presentation
of brute straight
St. Raight, himself
"as head strong as an allegory on the banks of the Nile".

Auntie Poetic's pleasure is *never* done
in a purely new frame, a shift is always
a dirty trick
of memory and the nepotism of error's constant
scramble *for* signs,
even as *for* is one of two
faces with three expressions, and contradiction's posing
why, all-whys
exposes the *why out!*: Hip crosses itself
with what it's cross at — the impulsive, jettisoning jet set
and the earth bound pulse-takers taking it with them.
O the too too dimensional universe lies here
in the black *plane*
box — *clique* of the angels
to heel. Hurry up,
let's get out of here, *here* comes

the melody.

Everytime I go into the two-door bathroom
to take a leak and mother walks in
to her bedroom or into the breakfast room
on the other side
I yell "I'm in here!" unless she yells it sarcastically first
but by this time I'm already already yet circumspectly
my own red carpet Layton precursor.

Something surplus in the usage
like in the not exactly corny or outdated "take a leak".

The way out of the pleasure priniciple
is not the phylogenetic *Turtle Diary*
journey to the entropic of uncancer.

Knowledge is true as it comes
back, catches you up
on things, not on itself as it explodes, tho that too,
intentions aside (we want to ape our cyborgs),
nor as transferred to Russell, childhood icon
now a reconstruction more alive limited than dead right
reified deified and than ear-marked whole-voiced.

Tho the speech parts of his life in a part of his life
were intended to cohere and wholly connect.

A whole argument stayed
clear
of now. Certainty cuts its losses in the foundation,
jumps into the superstructure, ties into the certainty
of the bomb. Sitting in the upside down rootless tree
in mid autumn with Hussurreal, my dog becomes so
intentional and that's just from my point-
of-view consciousness! Stabbed in the back
but *I* (don't slash *me*) do the twisting.

Next week: Spinoza, something on the emotions
and the more-than-one-door into historical explanation
according to Charles Taylor the philosopher,
not the race horse owner and friend of the "gadfly"
Scott Symons who reads our politics from Morocco
and in the way we walko
or, in a move that out-penetrates doctrinaire fifties
Mailerian hip, ironically put out
of the human gestalt the more
a good word
is put in for it,

reads at least the politics our "clavicles" deserve
(with a condescending blanket good word for "straight"

Albertans, reformer "time of her time" Albertans).
Hip, ie hip hip hooray for the Family Compact and how
it squares with the more roccoco gaits of perception.

Left right left right, two Charles Taylors vote with their feet.
Neither a superstructural borrower nor a base lender be
but above all else
know that in the keep-
your-Hussurreal-in-
order, there are no doors, funny frames yes but no doors,
especially of perception. Dig a little pit for the mares
because Northern Dancer, tho eager, is not too tall.
"Sex 'n' Death" rides again.

The modern self digs a little hole in time
out of time, deliberates in its Hussurreal plane then ex-
plains its submarine *fatal* position in Tennessee
with the non-locality angles of the bp bp beep
porpoiseful periscope of innocence,
like the pricked balloon prick of an ambigandsmalluous whale.
In the fuse-flare rush hour
an *epoche* intimates epochal horizon —
if they still have such a thing
out there tumbling with Archimedes.

Name the year Kroetsch, Wiebe and Metcalf
all had literary bowel movements?
Kroetsch's was the most artsy, Wiebe's the most regular.
Metcalf's the most fartsy, actually soft porno running off
the page el disgusto, and perhaps a year later on the radio.

Dorf in a dark mud farted, "shitting a little, possibly".
Surfacing, the writing can't decide, flush
with the physiological uncertainty, itself flush, but unflushed,

with the mud — that through and through surface —

what gives.

CRYOGENIC THOUGHT

After the reading I listened
to some jazz guitar advertized as jazz guitar
but which was not always. Doughnuts, wine and coffee
plus a glass of black licorice twisters for refreshments.
A woman and two children waited for a chance, then left
after a poem before a poem but not before they hit
the refreshment table again. I turn the radio on in
my mother's Taurus for which clash at this time
of writing the new buzz word 'oxymoron' comes to mind
since it's used
increasingly as confusingly but reflexively as "no
pun intended". I listen to the CBC jazz with hands on
the leather steering wheel. Why am I tense future tense,
switching tense? I relax and lean over, right over
the armrest. Coalhurst
we smugly thought a dirty little village has now no coal
but is bedroom to Leth- not Lethe-bridge, lit up more,
with a big restaurant just off
the highway. It's all so "postmodern" not neo-modern Bruce
F. calls the responsible(?) step back from being
implicated. Leather jazz and sodium vapour
at all
the highway turn offs and cross-fingered
overpass, intersection of #3 and 23. My hand clasps a cold
green golden delicious apple on the seat. Apple sitting (apple
hanging out) for a couple of days on the seat in the garage,
nestled in the corner the armrest makes. Nestled in a flight
of surplus equilibrium. Nestled just beyond the nest egg
of everybody's auto-biographical, endless in-fractions.
Now it *is* out of the bag. The wooden figurative "woodwork"
as in "out of/of the" possesses me. I wrote a cheque
for a million dollars for each of a bunch of fellow students
in grade twelve. I thought I was
onto a breakthrough (O, orientation) concerning

financial matters and tested my faithful understanding
the cheques
needs must bounce. But then I secretly wanted them all back.
I didn't know clouds at all.

Coming out of the woodwork is so suggestive especially without the quotation marks. But yet lives up to *wooden* the way abstractly I play with the idea. *Wooden* is perfectly flipped appropriate. I should say screwed down or up the spiral more.

The speeding bullet, the speeding ticket I got later on
two miles from Nobleford. A fragment or a full sentence.
A bag of 7 for 11 videos and one loose apple, apple loose ah, upsetting itself in the tight horsepower cart. Speeding home to catch the midnight movie on the CBC channel. I don't want to divulge the nature of the government
cheque but for four dollars equal to the speeding ticket. Here I have a small political unconscious, one of many, that creeps up on me, not quite referring to taking the bus going north to Calgary, Edmonton or Banff.

From the woodwork on the bus everthing comes, so much freed up to read (look suicidally sideways for a long stretch of seconds) of the imagination dangling its fingers in
the water or naughtily for your own lessening sense, the big tractor tread. The bus is a little more existential the way it rudely pulls into the small towns and you see what you wouldn't have bothered to chance fly to predictable contour. Fiction roaring and fluttering as vantage points arriving at back doors at a disadvantage with abandon, which see back only a terminally lost and lonely contingent. Anybody might get on. It could go either way, you might be tempted to snap it, accelerate it charm, a quantum leap backward. I got on once in a full fare, fairly full bus, was stuffing my coat into the overhead
rack and suddenly knew my fly
was down. Instead of just seating down zip I put my coat

under my chin and fumbled obviously under it. This isn't
quite true but sort of a self-perceptual blending
to feeling equivalent. I don't mean to be coy or old fashioned
either. McLuhan thought you could only get so expressive
which usage expresses how Marshall could slip into the one
dimensional tac tic just as the culture environment toes
a line. But it's not coy, it's a standard, crotchedy old tune
everybody recognizes. So many sing what they hate is catchy.
It's two-thirty now and Winston Churchill the guinea pig, not
the painter, has taken me like a vampire.

Coming out of the woodwork is an embarassment of riches
and yet I don't know how to work it in with all its Blakean
potential. That's not the lacquer talking. The liquor gets
the locker a larynx, goes from structure to force expressly.
Elves Expressly. Little green love me medium rare.

"Bullshit" does not offend except it is known to mean to,
so does, pop, two teenage boys were thrown off
the bus for "vile language". (I ask "language itself?")
The phrase "kids really" has a dramatic, creepy and creeping-
in force. It is some other movie, in a permanent coma.

Floating along in a bus is intimating two landscapes passing
in the broad daylight, the one you bring, the one that comes.
Time intercoursing spaces with unnatural derivatives of
instantaneous memory and desire. A condom on wheels called
Trojan. Did Helen / launch a thousand brand names?
The horse was as much Greek to me.
Which side of the envelope the letters are applied to
is a pleasant confusion somehow misconceived.

The stink of sugar beet pulp used to be a much bigger thing
not when they raised cane tariffs but subsidized the beets
more. Picture Butte and Taber had huge sugar factories.
My sister wanted to go to Picture Butte for a holiday, just
Jungian idea my father thought. Horse drawn towns spaced
out by the CPR, dream of kids half broke sky broke flat broke.

Sometimes I see a skull and crossbones
on a New York Yankees ball hat.

The bus driver shakes his finger at the two, his voice rising
to "vile language". Quotation marks are all that's left
after they get off. The driver is a pedestrian in his own bus.
I'm pointed south, he's pointed north. I was too far back
to hear but I know my type and believe the allegations.
It's a simple ticket I speedily recover.

School lets out / a karate yell, the school problem seems
to be latent kicking and screaming no matter how you
graduate it, world class notwithstanding.

The pavement I imagine never felt so good at the wrong time.
The two kids reeling, study not the bus but the long gesture
they can't get out of.

I ate the apple but through a tactile stylization I imagined it
a coconut. Nobody's feelings were hurt by my fantasy as
I went back over to apple in a controlled slide. Have-a-lunch
in the ball park of your hunger.

A bunch of deep womb allstars heading south on no. 2. Hi
ways revisited are more surplus value for romantic skimming
and more diminishing returns on the run on the milk way
of getting there when you're disciplined-in with other here-
engraving *daseins* from all over. Commanding a late winter
mountain sunset, I put my fiat up. Mistaking an abandoned
farm house with its fiery windows for a snug feeling you
meet halfway is good medicine for sleeping around without
thinking. Got to be woodwork as much for arrival as
departure. A cliché is not a frozen heart but a cry-
ogenic thought. A TV dinner without a TV is sweeter than
preservation but not than tantalus. McLuhan says truth is
contraction *and* expansion. Ain't that the truth, *vermouth*
wormwood. Brevity is the soul of a halfwit. Wyndham/Lewis
Mumford both said when the mind is creative it gets
an erection, Mumford getting it from Sir Patrick Geddes who

localized the erection in the brain. Before Sir Patrick, "O
where shall I find", would come to mind
I thought I was looking for a name with inferior connotations
because it was 19th century and I hadn't, the dross lost,
heard of it before Lewis — I presume Nobleford. My mother
lives in: Mumford is the word. All those uses of 'emasculate'
are slowly feeling not so confident. One man's base irony is
another person's putting not too fine a point on it. Not so
confident even when in positions usually so defensible,
and what's more, proactive.

Got in an argument with someone once as to whether it was
Lewis Mumford or Mumford Lewis. I was right and knew it.
But just now I thought of a dying man who only had dying
words saying "Mumford Lewis" and leaving it at that knowing
it was wrong, as a harmless, completely private revenge
on a hypothetical public revenge, of not the wronged
but the wrong answer.

Woodwork is hurting them for their own good. Be
the pressure that squeezes your arm. Velcro Lips turned out
to be truth in a time capsule. Dr. Strangelove,
the woodwork ha! / s a runny nose.

Walk down the hall a thousand times. Ambush is too killdare,
in bed with a nurse's cold too catchy. Graffitti is flush living
dead, wooed a-mirror. Still don't see this wood thing working.

You pay the policeman a compliment but spell it with an 'e',
you the little government, for the people you let him let you,
fall guy, deadwood mood expanding beyond the social contract.
If thick could kill, eh. Condensing to the letter gives off.

He knows you're the boss. According to the letter you've said
nothing. You cave in completely (I guess "you" is saying
"put yourself in my negation!") (Or I guess the law has caught
me up as it bends through an-aught and into a more would-be
you). It becomes a consolation when he realizes he's
answered all his own questions. The letter of the law

suddenly overstepping itself. The mood is your right.
It goes up his nostrils directly to the brain. You did nothing
at this epiphenomal level, a grievous connivance. The crime
is now taking place in full view and he takes it like an addict.

You shrink to a vicious psychiatry. He puts on a brave
pleasant tree. The woodwork is stunned.

Leona Gom wrote one of her first stories around getting
a sliver in her finger. She was divinely right. I've fallen
on hard times. Once you've been inspired, caught the common
poetry cold, it's all ice flows, sweating the impossible.

The woodwork is starting to look like a school of fish.
Stanley Fish. Is there a Nietzsche in Aladdin's genealogical
lamp? I'm half quoting myself and half someone else.

I pedal the metal. I don't know if Glenn Gould would
have liked the action, I feather my letting go. While the rpms
climb up diagonally in rectangular increments next to fixed
numbers the bigger numbers on the computer screen
geometrically transmute in and out of each other. A diagonal
up and down illusion runs through its worried undecidable
face. "It" is my impressive velocity, traceably "my" edgy id.
My structurated ego accepts the born-to-be-ripped ticket
and approaches escape projection. The windshield is F-U-ll
of flashing light. I parachute in with a rewrite. If I were
Woody Allen my career, because I wouldn't really be Woody
Allen, would progress in exactly the opposite direction.
You'd have to have your Bergman first so you wouldn't end up
in *Wayne's World*, at least too soon. *Take the Money and Run*
slowly.

In the *Misfits* Marilyn Monroe moves into a half house.
The woodwork is all suffering animals, Clark Gable is
the roof, drunk on the hood of his truck, younger than his *Not
In Our Genes* children filling their boot straps with Aut-ry,
the bigger-than-baseball-"Ya bums" owner, living in their
Sir James [J]eans' "everybody unfree but me."

America is not getting along in real life here. (In *Tombstone*
's docu/holi-day voice-over, "Tom *Mix* wept" at history
's cutting room crossroads funeral when Christ was a cowboy
with his upright Whyat bio on his chest, and when humourous
epitaphs played into *resurrecting* industry.) Some who
say it's all stars now, the astronomical kind, re yur paradigm,
say in the movies it's getting brighter but like a nova express.
"Yur" concedes how the edge comes off a serious usage.
"Paradigms Lost", "Can you spare me a paradigm?"
Spare me . . . I should say. "Yur" is an embarrassment too,
concedes the losses haven't been cut. "Poetic" phenomenology
is a convention, a rhetoric whose potential is
so fine it could be violated by all "ideas". "Any" ideas?

In my rear view mirror I can see the cop with his cap off
writing out the ticket, light shining dimly on his bald head
under the flashers on the roof. He's more active now that his
cruiser is stopped. The momentum of the machinery is un-
affected. I'm special, a joy apart / for him. I'm all drugs.
The privatization of public duty. When he cleans his uniform
he blends into his job of which the speed of its light
is constant even though his effort as a citizen
seems as cautionary as my aching, heavy foot.

Bearing down on the both of us is a vehicle with only one head-
light. A small revenge/excuse in my heart watches his bald
bent-over head, shining dully through the windshield.
At a bookstore reading in Lethbridge I met the woman who cuts
my brother's hair. At the U of L she'd been studying *Finnegans
Wake* at night. She recognized the pattern on the doublin'
pates, I asked her baldly, rhetorically and I spin at the proper
syntax here as I sentence myself.

I pick up my policeman and point it at the blushing one eye
no doubt homeopathically slowing as well as hurrying by.
Justice is not blind or too general but too much of an over-
tonic physics, not to warp away.

Breaking the law, breaking fast, *velox* bull-arena dances around the charges. The geo skip of whiz words. Structures collapsing under their own weight is a common observation. Much so-called criminal behaviour is more reactionary than the held-up law. Working with a deficit teleology is more purposive than dead weight. Emotions rush the woodwork.

In the gym in Banff Steve the bouncer teases Jerry the cop who sits on a bench staring at the wall, taking too long between sets. I do skeletal workouts, ie 1/2 hour. Steve does full bodied ones, ie 2 or 3 hours. Jerry's shift changes all the time. We spot one another on the bench press, one finger makes up the difference. Walking home I feel about this high, a human X-ray machine.

My dog thinks I'm an accountant. I can't remember what "staring out of the woodwork" means now. Gertrude, like her brother Ein, was right about her relative observer. My dog is a catchall retriever, bona fido Bradbury. "Invisible architecture" so a latest universe Galatea*sed* the prodi-gal tears just as hyper poetry knocks off another nano near miss exercising the right, its huffing shadow. Radical hypocrisy turns the other half in — to Copernicus for all seizings. Generic expectation trip-ups. Then monkey's peduncle assumption. The wall of static message undertaker. *Uber* over, radio-wise.

Belief is observable. My dog believes in "hockey ball", "piddle", "walk". In the bathroom she lies in wait, I sit and plate. I reach for the roll, she wipes the slate/with me. Nice to be wagged, put in the ken. Here's to *Hegel's Vacation* and Nietzsche's puddle bath. Horse hug down the recap hole. Jack-of-all-trades back in the forgotten umbrillo box.

Her tail softwares my jacket on the floor when I'm standing right there. Is it my armpits recollected in tranquility? Or I'm wearing a telegram, which isn't a woodwork metaphor but an important, buried analogy? This from-far-away-and-past-telegram is useless but a pure pleasure I guess. Mind you I've never taken wagging-tail immersion. A working sniff in the field is wont to typify the ground like police flashers. Honk if you love McLuhan.

She composes me like the cop, each nails me to the wall, each makes me wanted, not feel wanted. Both have laws. I can't get beyond the detail-tailing fields which break in every point of departure as before we now know by — "gangsters more than anyone affirm the categorical imper/ative" with addendum subtracting themselves. Their guilt simplex twists the non-totaling manifest of the arch ark of America's Marx Brother-hood, calls up "in or out" destiny slave-whole to the flag up. Exclude-me-in showbiz captures freedom for the other half-masters. In debrief, the re-entry

We / st — cracking itself with both AI's after the law
and the hand that feeds it return on one another
as the snake and its tail, as insinuated Z[ero]thustra
chokes on its head till he bites and swallows
so freedom and the law become one
along a new axis, alt[a]r-straight on the feedback — cubistic
and counting in the contrails' thrust parodies. The tense
action/reaction stagger the present and sunspots
break the immediate magnet of the Oedipal wall.

She wears a black hole on her sleeve. That's as bad as talking about the woodwork. My sleeve is the great wall in outer space. Is that a comforting characterization? But it mattered to Buber who was kicked out of his house before the Nazis actually kicked him out, and it almost killed him by his own hand till Kant saved him, removed again, with *out*-of-mind space and time.

She twists her head at every threshold we direct into her invisible house. Her black hole is oblong and wobbles, is big on belief, short on Whitehead, Alfred magnetic North.

We subscribe to a mutual condensation. Prehistory of
a family except for the oblong face she wears on her sleeve,
many of the melancholies it shifts kinemorphs to.

A black hole wobbles between my shoulder and my elbow,
a face weighted-in with God and then -down for Godot in its
secondary motion, not yet practised up between families
where a decision can float like a knuckle ball randomly
and pretty: near timeless, the kind of action a pianist
fluttering backward into previous notes could appreciate
as the haunted better voice.

Something has to be done, what is done is abandoned.
Up close the world is Dewey. We're not all furtive Johns.

Smith walks by Brown's front window, sees the young female
Labrador on two legs humping the back of Brown
who is apparently sleeping on the couch.

Smith is a fiction. Brown is me. The Labrador seems
not to know the difference. I don't disabuse her.

The family breaks into the mercury of little poisons. Is that
Bronx talk? In the game I play with the dog she's unforgiving.
I'm stuck in the great wall. She reflects me into the glue
and the gluons. I can laminate a nation all I want. A sing-
ularity is yclept, not "eclipsed", "God." A singularity
only promises a universe garden was Kant's anti-idea of art.

One of the meanings of 'quantized' which is generally speaking
user-friendliness par excellence, is the idea of the total numb
er of electrons. If you ignore the little mothers of all
mornings after and, if you'll excuse the English on it, some
smashing reconstruction. Just now a half-ton passed my base
-ment window in Banff here and another one going the other
way. Intended out like that they looked like a giant
two-winged bird, the usual kind, a stationary event
which flashed and faded.

The sun seems on the one hand only wit and then dimly true
to a frightening degree. Back to Leona Gom's sliver,
Lou Salomé said "It almost seemed to me as if
anything one touched *correctly*, would lead one to the centre
of things", re her lack of aims and ambition. Also
quantization is the trick-all of melody, Max Planck's minimal
sawdust discretely fudging such wooden strains. Is being
good, Aristotelian, ie an achievement, or mostly
the repression of desire, the long modern cliché? Upbringing
on balance leaves us / a little extra. You get a charge
out of being good. What we inhabit and create as extra
is a woodwork, when we step into what would work. On TV
all these personalities banally pontificating on how banal
Neil Armstrong's first words from the moon were.
On the other side of the light barrier those tacky tachyons
cancanning big time. With gravitas I think I'll stick
to one small step. Frank Davey says the first person plural
is phoney, and worse, the language of authority. The first
person *rural* has backup to burn, unless with striking match
met and synchronous misprision she fires herself, back when
puns split trunks, were too clever by half.

When the little changes we-in-situ generate are trained into
a we-state electrical projects that light up a nation are not
possible but actually a moon. We wax about it while you and I
are fazed by the dark. Its gravity runs right through the living
rooms. One small step and you're fit to be tide coming in
watching the subliminal death bubbles of a slow motion levity.
You shrink back not into the incompleteness theorem
but the crater of first impression.

Here I am in the bus double parked at a traffic light. A regular
knuckle ball as I peek over to see what this woman is reading
when she folds her hand into her closed book. I guess I'm mor-
ally neutral at this time, revving my engine. On the other hand
handing over our wrongful potential enjoins we're at least bad
predictably. Cheated desire makes you horny. It's romance
that smells something, makes a killing. Giant steps are a

multinational floating that never steps down. I shat into my
new black and white cowboy boots around the poplar tree
I was tied to. If I had my choice it would be between those
little boots and a giant escape. Thank God God is a God
with a vengeance . Peirce says time itself is not temporal.
Is there any relation between Job, who found God a beautiful
brute who gave no quarter, even at the end, to the fiscal year,
and the other pronunciation "jobs jobs jobs" which
according to *Random* has no etymological origin?

"Neolithic lithographic" is a phrase I've salvaged from somewhere else. None of the *Morningside* media column panel
knew what "begging the question" meant, including Robert
Fulford who luckily, he said, had never used it. If an author
should stay away from authority how humble is it honest
to get? New authority comes in small packages. Or better
yet, as not quite free advice. Certainly free but not quite
advice. My advice is you / run intentional interference
because you can't / help yourself. Go hard *and* easy on those
enjambments. Liquidate with stream prejudice, pragmatic
dice playing the role of the walk-on part
of the water. Con-fuse the dynamite with wiry, why-are-we,
bleeding, nothing-like ohms. Why bank on the en-chanted,
still river? Deficit D-E Nile is to remember Joyce's ABC
echo-logic, his pyramid run on the great givers run through
the hands like all-state knowing through the no-state,
agent origin. The etymology of 'interpret' interprets itself,
if it were a self and not simply the undoing of the donned
dawn. *To do* is the rolling explanus. A bore is born,
with useless tits and arrows. The C.$. Pursed self
is the arch *to err*, and in arrears, not inner ears. Not
by breed alone. My dog is definitely not a hate mongrel.
Re the exposure of breasts in *The Globe and Mail* (July 17,
1992) Kimberley Noble is not related (to me). Re libel chill
will we ever know what her book exposes of the Bronfman
current accounts (now the mov/ing credits), not the Richler
booze, um past?

BLANCH IN FRANCE

Another old girlfriend he learns. Has gotten married.
"Solves that." As if / uneasy rider were an ingrown stone
and "Don't Goethe that joint" a fate avoided
according to Ortega, but that lanced by Nicholas Boyle's
Poetry of Desire. The sublime ends in bent over embers, ooze
and snooze. A great bubble phallusy gone
and everthing remains pathetically "search me".

A sophisticated piece of farm equipment
from an American manufacturer achieves a kind of orbit
in the Canadian prairies. Coming out of the yard in road gear
it's an invading army. In the field it sinks, rusts where it
shines. Cognate to the heart part pumping blood up
a couple of feet to a shock absorber, reiterating motor,
absorbent homeostatic cloud or bolt
embedded in pre-Christian tolerances, thinly veiled
temper, thinly veiled fool's kite. Even then her brain
was PhD as it so soberly analyzed the brains
that were pickling around us. Got Jimmy to the hospital
three or four hours before his massive heart attack,
against his will.

Farming is multiplied through the economy and subtended
by export enhancement programs. Sometimes comes right
off the ground by GATT or by Mahatma Gandhi. Or somebody
mentions your name on the radio. A name much like yours.
Then diseases are periodized on the computer and presented
as products. Germ plasm is screen-tested
onto a chemical spectrum alter-logo'd by a transnational.
Superpork geneticized into slaughter shoes. Off
the highheeled debut cooked. A hawk screams above/below
the diesel, dialectic at least in the height of these craven
prepositions. You pick out an old gestalt, a lobotomized
gestalt, or rather the opposite, a controlled experiment,
a multiple of a skeletal ecology cycle. Sun activity

that affects your field/plan
like a Minerva-shot art movement fifteen years later.
An old gestalt raced through by new, confounding intentions,
different breeds of signs run through the same regulator.
Different initial conditions further apart down the road.

Would a combine make you laugh if the table auger sang
German lieder while the sieves fiendishly masturbated?
Lightning can still seem mean-spirited. Just behind the knife
on the front of the swather table into the life
under the canopy of canola plants turnip breath prevails
and a swarming town square or in another inappropriate way
ie not appropriating but a dislodging
into the tell-a-graphic alienation required against it,
a campus in the fall from a reunion point of view,
or an entomologist promoting insects on the radio
or camping one up to his kids in bed, the different gaits,
the gaudy colours of hard-edged bugs, the quantum leap sizes
of worms and caterpillars, the bustle, the comedy of so many
endings, the laughter of a god with half a brain,
the smear campaign of scar fate
rubbed right out from under your lightning-nailed fingers
now in a jerky science movie, archeology of Charlie neurons
in separate grooves in far off parallel to your striated nails
as if they were synthesized in respect to crude recurrences
till dynamics make them infinite reminders or remainders
if you like equilibriums kiltered into qualities of mind.
Only superman's psychological, essence of blue,
lovesick period knows for sure. Gossip is God-sip and Hugh
kennered Lewis, ie Wind-ham, regaled old Pound
with Old Possum's misery. Jesus butt. The whiff of sandal,
the wife of bath, bottom student. Then everything scratched,
senses parlayed, here three senses of 'over'.

Still you get the idea. A junkie overcomes sex. See kernels
piling up in the hopper. With one finger you peel away
the dirt till you till moisture, then the stut/tered seed
doubly taken, once for luck, twice for the micro story
to deform the instant symmetry, not like a little sculpture
in a diaper, more like a grass hopper leg, considered, zig zag
on white paper, unlike a rubbed-in butt. A kid stayed

her first whole day in school. Dirty nails in the morning
till the experiments came and the 4H horse's hide
crawled into husbandry with a ground-figuring wink.
By the afternoon she had academic standing
and her nails were growing new margins.
Of error she bore flight paths, flailing away
into a negative capability
wrong-righted by a cult / ural monologue
collapsing surplus into necessity
fostering children in the prescinded periphery
middle distance, ironizing the Vygotsky zone
into afterworlds of chasing after
between-time, which was, awkward, touching
(thrown-out actual metaphor with the right
without-brackets bracketed touch living on after
in a temporizing and phantomized para-zero
Zeno moment), now continuum-primed and pinealized,
now delyricized unZwicky zoo.

Adult children uphold by their negative self-images
the partially decontaminated hegemony
because "dieselled" centreless and full
of introjected schizoids breeder-reacting a fuseable con-
science. The saving sun bomb Gaza uplift, tamed name
of blindness, is kiltered into the ground. Math ascends
and desires the dirt, infantilizes and super-foundationally
incompletes it. Porno Zeit-zit tree-fractals
the telio-fleshold. For-the-forest backdoors still drop
emergent governor gates. And swing the charm, gives us
a start, immediately pun-collapsed into mediated freedom

determinants. History by diminishing imaginaries.
Ruthless, moulting hope sublimated without repression
but into the ataraxia of wave-absorbent potato eyes, site
unseen in Vico-creep trans-identities. The clean grain
auger it's called. Yet the seed goes to the seed
cleaning plant before you seed it next spring.
A couple of tons of steel, a twelve ply tire holds it up
in the front. The v-edged packers press the dirt, seed seeded,
like a nut in chocolate. A hoe bed adjusted like an opinion
poll, hits the moisture as a trendy contourist. The new
mathematics of result lowers you back down
in the well of beans, you get the idea again when you hear it
on the noon show.

A remembered gestalt no matter what
sophisticated catalyst you insult it with is sentimental.
You manipulate your sample. Otherwise it's worse. Change
the station *of course*.

The right idea is a bigger body than ever
in the machine whose volume is machined by other machines
according to specs the Gnomes of Zurich use or wear. Neither,
it's all in their leg bones
which mostly achieve an easy equilibrium
sometimes overdrawn, sometimes too big for their desks'
slide-out keyboard boards.

Supper is beyond "how was it?" You burp for a couple of hours
and lunch is doing you like dropped acid
behind the wide waiting blink till organs parse and Valery
their numb numbs. Underwear is sweaty and brown.
Everything converges on your dirty body. It needs gaskets.
It's got gas guts. A baby body that won't quit. The clothes
are big and create nakedness, roughly. Degree of dungaree,
I, song of my sing. The combine seat is tested till furrowed
farmers go ratsy. You soil yourself some more,

glow in the dark and the beard doth grow. A sensation
of warmth against the air conditioner. You resist it
like an east wind and look at the quilted work shirt
under the sun which is low on fuel. A loose connection
in "the sun . . ." Even anger works the way the coffee stays
warm behind the gear shift, actually almost stuck
wedged in there.

Rash to say diaper. Feel your clothes a lot, cool, pulled
on the top of the thigh, hot and sweaty in the pants' ass.
Id loves the repressed-up clearcut trinity twin
from the demon mine. Refined, ele-mental body hate.
Heat from the vent makes the anger dysfunctional. Kick
a window, pull a lever too hard, changes in the biochemistry.
Mouth dry. Breathe with a slight heart pain. Might as well be
naked, touch your temperature. Hide your hide
in damn clothes, good clothes though
sometimes the right idea.

The instrument panel, test pattern in the dark,
extract domestic over to your right, little lights
like in the sky. You'd say 'heaven' in this sty
before you'd say 'heavens' in the new archaic plural.
The heavy glass wrapped around in front shows lights
not there but behind you. Mixed in with the stars. In the King
Eddy in the summer in the afternoon. Dim bar shimmers.
Sadder or simply radiant leaving a bar in the early, lite 3.5%
evening. Jon said in the dimmer shimmer he would go
for "Afternoon Starlight". Title as heavenly adjustment
activating the higher unconscious
with the beatnik wishing on original sin — like to commit one.
The sun as star is a good concept shake. Snap telescope.
Funny how glitz can have lost it.

Flat boredom turns up an addiction that needs more
than night figured out by little lights. The night big on gone.
O believin' in oblivion. Belief is the constipated first person
even humped up to heaven near teratological Wall / ace

frozen in palmed-off rabbit pathology. The eliminationist,
accused excused into the third person,
says it never appears, dissolves just — in time,
too mobile and almost hydra yanging non-locally with doubt.
Radical yin chaos'd in the last detail
blown up to the always-himself-Nicholson flick import.
Not of an eye heaven but a constellation that can't hold
or hole up. The fat of the land so to speak carelessly.
The flat of mental reprise, musically speaking, financially
holding. Radical narcissism is more intersubjective
albeit subterranean, than do-goodism said a critic
against danger-us redemption. This confirmed on *Sunday
Morning*, the radio show slicing itself into big pre-emptions,
by an English cross-dresser. What did you
think of "come-you-ism" (pretty bad?), Mailer's
anti-communist pun said in a split-off Joycean voice.
Why Are We In Next Ear Country?

As of August 4th, 1992 we've had 13.8 inches of rain,
one of it in May, 6.5 in June miraculous to me, 46
to me at five or six, it takes me back to normal times
when I was a lush, not a precocious lush, just storing up
against the grain. Finally! the summer-heated-hated west
wind, actually cool today and cooler again this evening
as I walked back into town or an electric cactus
sublating itself with lights, rootless cheer, with itchy wind,
hot or otherwise, like being in somebody's bosom again
though not as beyond nostalgia as that, a stiff cutting
nostalgia, present, then equal and opposite, if the truth be
known. Also a skunk amid the montrous rustling crop
stuck its head out black and white in the dim light.
I stepped on it, I mean got running
for the sake of one of those spoiled dogs I have and her aux-
iliary space that reminds me the best adults are kids
and so are some of the worst or should I say
some of our best mom/ents are acting as such.

Relate your alien smell to the sinking in that occurs to you
at both ends of the dirempted mind. The illusioning mind
makes the illusion of mind work, till we sort it out,
like "the stars older than the universe". To be disillusioned
is to recognize you're living in and as a prototype
ill designed, now de-signed. To be cancelled now is to be
returned to air. To be folded is the winter of our discontent
but ghosts generalize the battle. My hawked kingdom,
on pins, even at these desperate points, is cast broad
and plays at different times. Without the media news is
a great code. My horse! for something in between. Cognition
escapes and misprisions you. Late twentieth century genitals
are the pre-eminent foreign bodies
parasitic on the just normally possessed chiasma of flesh.
John Glassco remembered Show-pen-how-are-ya!
who said the conscious falling rock would will itself to fall,
and would be right.

Hi, how ya doin, double exposure, triple E Galipoli, Barbary
states of the state, would you care to comment on that
formula prime minister, inevitable godsend I mean godlend
I mean good land for the sake of the children, no not
the children, again but rather the fluid formula, creative
book keeping but just how inevitable and just how just ice
will melt thank children for playing into their hands
played out. The rest, is dreaming history, praying into
a real dive. Ears plugged into the mouths of not babes
dummy but next over, past the Klein bottle
(not a topical reference circa the Alberta "revolution",
but a topological one circa "aboutness", withdrawn really)
to the Klein dolls that, proleptic traces of 'glamour'
and old spells inscribed in the spelling,
grammarize the barbary gestures.

Say bye to Blanch in France. Mayonnaise on apple for not
a people's poet buried in a series of half equations sliding
back from the end of the regulation wobbling pivot. Miracle
Whip. Pound the falcon cannot hear the falconer Stevens

and pounds around Europe. Wallace puts his feet up on a bird
bath and sucks at exotic combinations of imported foods
(and a German book). The assurance of death, the moment
of accidence. Art sinks Dalmatian teeth into the TV cabinet.
One friend in New York, one in London, me in Nobleford,
a great circle triangle, the naked ape in Nobleford overflows
8 million mega-geists, Ulysses, ie Rawhide radio, hosts
the folksinger's English rodeo dog. That's a lot of methane
butane Scottish post card coos, a little expression, please!

Blanch in France come in, just taking a leak, small stream,
got me by the stalls, purchase the onions, tears, tears before
the popcorn, tears à la Chomsky deep down but no Tennyson
for your punk chemism. Concepts ex / ceed impartially,
partially disown metaphors. 'Root' sur-faces in the fresh
desert, here sur-real is not necessary in the straight outside
root irony — as opposed to the irony of the circular route.

He called me silly on the air, she called me silly till she
righted herself. By that time I was head over heels.
He coined me on the CPR tracks. We, the braid of I's,
have to live it up to it, now, as well as look it up. She called
me on the foreign debt. If we have to look it up we might
as well go empire or up in vertical miles
which are longer at first then shorter, even
as the Russian spine apple-up-sees another 3 or 4 inches
under the cosmic lack of surveillance. A lot
of my first world heroes have wobbled into social revision
and are better persons for it. In a small way I wish
I could say "better men for it" just for the contentless
usage click, though notice the thrust of the meaning,
ie the reformed and contented-with lack of thrust. Outside
of the respective moral termini, why is an "asshole"
acting twitty more charming than a twit acting vulgar?
Beyond goodness and a mere bulldozing *why*,
is this a question of the twit disease? Is Hamlet
the perfect asshole twit?

I need something to correct to get going, I say in an anti-
progressivist spirit which is a form of progress
that has to be swallowed harder and brought up again
like kids and ?what do you do with them
when the handling charges are out of reach
of handling your charges. At least it makes you think
this way about larger issues. The thin edge of wedgucation
started back in the pre-industrial age. Thomas Merton
started the Second World War. History is kidding without
a cause, no end insight. I've been wrong all along becomes
all right sixties exclaim for me personally writing it up
as the continuum-of-wedge kid skates trans-epochally
and harvests me prematurely. The aggregrate great kid theory
of finish yourself. Came upon a rich man's disease,
borne-in-the-air disease, art disease borne in Bethune's
art disease cut to the quick, the film, the watch that ends.

The I's are dropping out of the we glazed on the satellites,
no one's in the saddle, the eagle has landed
just when Citizens Band Macpherson redefined property
as caught in the immigrant/emigrant shuffle demons
at the level of voice, pitched at home but living it up to it,
never landing now that the gentry's re-entry is topsy
of the *Morningside*, Earle Birney's first ranch,
author of *Turvey*. Now the air is terra fermé,
now the infinite holes prepared to meet the infinite holes
are plugged. A stoical dog is easier to part with, in a sense,
than a spoiled one — if they can be born spoiled?
The metal table rattles because she trembles
when they clean the scent glands in her anus.

Fly by night ski why did you not tell me it was re-ritualized
family starspeak bastardized McLuhan anyway, middle earth,
meddle ages, the philosophy of right is in reverse,
two swords sans men crisscross up the stairs,
the UN seats by this logic itself down on Mars, the wars
being not lost on us. A vote goes into outer space, never
stops counting, no quasi crystal but back to the swollen sick

singularity, sick out of the wall of the other universes
like the wall before the end of the marathon
where runners enter the jelly, self and image unglued,
and leave their wills in consensual gravitons. No matter
how thorough you dry your hands
the side of your little finger is still wet when you slide it
over the page writing. This trivial "praxis"
(pace a D. Arnason character) hazard cum (pace my correct-
able self) superstition, is the beginning of dialectic,
the swinging kind, with the curli-cue addendum that it's not
the superstition but the corrupted will to camp it
that constitutes the torque. Always it's the limp

and blurring convolutions of the contrails
that figure instead of the goal, like Alan Borovoy
the civil liberties bachelor (because "before women
's liberation" re an honest dialectic of will and willingness)
who concentrates on making things less worse
(*Summerside*, "music of my life"). The clarity is never
in the buried exactitude or accordion brevity
and then new breath. It's in the constant/comment
that drowns itself out in the willowy shallows,
the body of work, of play, the extended body running to water
colours, the head floating on the hot springs,
Kroetsch's *Alibi* eyes stung open in the steam.
The nod comes back, goes elsewhere
over the cup of pre-empty square clapped down
on the drawing board. The floating-clear heads cut off
along the crossbar from the crucifix T's, and the Titanic acid
rises. The beard scratching and itching, neither a beard
nor a close shave but growing on indefinitely after the death
of a bunch of instances (reminiscent of M's title,
who said the beards in Edmonton going grey are being cut off).
Not chic macho, no overplay, no underplay. Slop the pig.
Bristles on the chin part of the brain. Going a little fungoid
after each yawn.

I'm a sucker for others' houses esp-ecially if they have lamps
on. Definitely a costume party. The windows are like fire
places and that's the burnt-out essence. I like to float
embers of exception Septembers flip. Overlook their mi-
graines, a slight hex in the kitchen, a hard book in the light
bath, the ring-around bath of light, make that a dull,
necessary book, a buzz of physical vision
eating into the edges of the pages. One of the James gang
on the couch out of the picture, old but hep to the young
"conquistador" Freud, slips to the brother
identified and analyzed by someone from Yorkton, S'wan.
Georg Lukács reappears to condemn the movie *Barton Fink*
which vapourized a realism cooled down to the four elements
of which fire emerged as the hero, cool as a cue-cumber-
some card, like fire is good people, heavy unbearable people!
The irony is the real's not turned on
as in "eat what's on your not plate". Rather the sacred is
as de-sacralized as the kink is alive! Irony works in strange
ways. Start here, the morning-after symbolist,
bankrupt realist writes in his synaesthetic arthritic hand.
Hard not to yawn a smile when the words come out
of his mouth in re-Cooper high neon.

Bruner says if deconstruction becomes an ex-
cess [*sic* — mete out the meat met as poison!]
(Thompson laughed and saw bobbing placards in the street
when I meant-shunned *Against Epistemology*) (Adorno
would neg/atively double up at 'demonstration',
ie cause'n'effect precluding the effective *cause*)
it yet began as a necessary switch from what to how
we know. Dennet says qualia across in this way evaporate.
Functions carry on. It's all garish Cooper-nican switches.
Eventually the anti-Hegelian's marginalized-as-material-
artefact predicament (Aristotle's word — shoot the translator
— for Kant's categories) fruitfly meets the absolute's gentle
persuaders, cognitive geneticists, where they hit you,
in the hardening of the habits. The socialist biologist

undercuts the basic sociobiologist not at the superordinate
or the subordinate level but right between the genus,
the most Aristotelian, the most novelistically rich. Right
where the middle brow wears his bottom line
or Hemingwayesque perpendicular, that open
experimental feeling.

You might say the mind-as-brain model is bloody
inadequate. But the only idealism you would want to muster is this veri inadequate ejaculation. Yet it's worse
than idealism, it's even the static, "no static", perspective
that forgets itself in homeostasis
whose wobble is a tranquil aggregrate of horrors or risks
if you bring back idealism as working for — meaning either
the path toward or the absent employer — change,
or working for pleasure which is as twisted as it seems
as it spirals into the paradigm of 'mutual exclusion', negated,
and ne-gated again, ie the hyperspace now.

It now being situated in the dirty dialogue,
actor's profession, pragmatic finesse, send me Red Grave
personified without a trace. The littlest hobo symptom
of the asymptote (math cheek turns the other into a nothing
butt) flees the flea, cusses the regulating Sir, over-intones
the original syntagm and dies into the answering service
only — like a regular divine comedian — to re-enter and dilate
the "genealogical lamp" — to raise the rub. The future
of identity sends its question-air,
the double hook of catch the breath
and catch *in* the breath in disorder to save
the received wisdom from itself. Beg me the lady,
a sorry state when the gilded Lily Tomlin convinces
the bag lady out of her cardboard. Remember her tiny,
not fitting the chair, and "and that's the truth"
which ever only haunts or falls
to the jumbled assizes of authority.

Coming down the hill on a cab-less swather
sits a young Hutterite with his shirt off,
black hair on his Laurentian pale chest.
In a quarter mile truck cruise you think of a former farm girl
gone city and what she would think now
touched off on chest hair (she did touch once on chest hair)
about the recesses of farm, then that woman you met
at the conference, how would she hold
the hairy farm life by the roots of the erotic. And before
you're even at the approach the praise due to another woman,
('due' shooting wildly back and forth, incorrectly),
tough/tender and transcending of her own character
assignation. Meeting her is extra spatial, down the road
and up the anti.

Then you're parked, the nubile daughter of a guy you were
jealous of and were meant to be, an inherent confusion,
new bile, humour as ugly laughter as laughter is the close-
to-the-kill industry of cavemen. Rides by on a bike,
pony tail, white shorts.

A twister walking up the driveway of the old railway station,
removed. A funnel cloud west of town during the hailstorm.
A tornado north near Lomond strikes up the gravel in the yard,
dissolves imagism on its way to the astro worm in the eye.

You are in the stomach on the ulcer probe video you,
little wipers under the cone of the granary
and the crop sucks in like all those badly infinite sub-zero
electrons pretty stand / ard pretty postulate pretty sprinkle,
also the bristly crystalized slime you were itching to get
puncturing puffs of anti-perfume. I'm always surprised
when someone hates me even though I'm always expecting it.
When you're considered / very nice it's hard to translate this
past the temptation to be so. Though left on your own
you are liable / to be just / so, which is a way of letting others
be primarily contemptible. A good dose of Augean stable
self-loathing blasts the misrecognition for all concerned.

This isn't pyschological or even religious self-loathing.
This is a post-industrial process to begin
predicting yourself against life-as-emptying-out,
the consumer unconscious, or the other version, life-as-
endless-apprenticeship. Tell me — is this romantic
or anti-romantic?

You may get better older
but better is leavings, banks, as in the private peripety
imparted to your new, time-nomadic pride of place,
chrysalis (U-haul word hull) of the Humean ego,
cicatrix of the eye tearing out to meet the all-the-same
flush. But also the sun and wind suck of the witnesses
who take the resistance you created for your character
they wormhole do — impressions of your impressions,
double negative as the positively you
indifferent to the pop-difference-enabled ego
as long as you leave it all behind, principally act
and deliberately never realize all the interest
you get out of you in a nice abnegative sense beyond
the genealogy of plumbing and plumping for a better *better*
trap, but not beyond the Idea of North
and sin-'n'-stir joker hoo-doo the spoonerism T. Eliot
hoodoo the conversion and the voices of the waste.

Comes in nine or certainly fewer than thirty, way fewer,
basic predicates, get a handle and how for this good infinity
we all swallow in. "Ego for sale!" is not logical
because the ego transcends the market. The ego transcends
period all the way in infinitesimally dot dot dot doting . . .
but then is like wealth, constantly in need of investment
and capable of synchronous suits, in fact well advised
to put everything into arms, not war or hugging self
and others but the vision of verbs at the tweed-dull end
of the tunnel of — love those tunnels love shatters
the features for the credits drawn on the features,
accelerated smash I've-been-everywhere hit by my own
incohereandtherency.

Lucky is the point these cornered sentences, this infinity
finding, soiled underwear, soil of the toil that toes like,
soil dirtied by confusion got religion, I mean your focus
goes chemical. Why would you want to go and read a book
like *Being and Nothingness* for anyway said a wife meekly
to a desolate husband looking over a desolate cityscape
(how have we learned this iconography we affirm
for a stairway and a song?) from their highrise
in a late sixties *Playboy* magazine singeing and singing by.
Early Peirce said hard is in the future. What do we do not
with binary functions but metaphor-adverbs,
"the sop to Cerberus", if the future condition lies
softly here? Rather than shoot the messenger
he tried to fall in love with the office supply manageress
dearest duress.

SLOE GIN SURPRISED US

Why is writing like — *sic*-ness —
like man (*sic*), same-*sic*-ing seeking — or / like
one of those garage hydraulic jacks,
your car six feet off the ground
on big phallic grease pole

or like the redundant "stool" that boosts you right off
the toilet seat, because it is not waste

but worse?

Often you run into it which presupposes it
gets away, which is a superficial attraction
about equal to the vague signal between your mouth
and your money
even if the uncoincident metaphor abstract
signalling coincidence
is taken in by those who would complete your sentences
with cocked heads only dogs can get away with
as our gestures are only midway mirrors we are
held in and, worse coincidence, for a dialogue's dropped power,
held *to*. Three cheers for the counter intuitions of math.

D.H., ie Diana Hartog Lawrence said Gerry Gilbert said
writing could be like strip mining.

It is certainly fateful
when it gets behind or under you.

It nags, makes your memory
too articulate and inevitable, gives your life piles too
of high centredness.

I hear lake water lapping
at the tobacconist's *racine*.

If this is all wrong and you can flip ahead
to your hermeneutic prow-ess which is the stern return
on your ignorance

ahead to a beating out of your always there
record-breaking, keeping heart, Nietzscheanly spare,
some weather, the ecstatic subsidence of nausea.
If Leo's trap claps, lyin's then thro teeth.

The pleasure in the unravished apple
transparent in the Nabokovian bowl
on the oakish Ikea fill —
in the blank there I feel free.

Flip to the eternal
mourning dove rite — the olfactory nerve
of the wine-dark apple equally beatifically buff.
"Wine-dark" is a crashing virus. Ezra had a virus or two.
(O these big mucky muck modernists
we dismantle, Esperanto!

But the Janus-*is* —
underpinning our pop hopes against pooped pope
hope. [In Hughes, Geo-ffrey's *Words In Time* (for anything)
we learn words
are the losses and false prophets of social history
retroactively rootless as they shift and even take
on opposite senses.
Of course they can turn back and become
self-fullfilling clean dirt
on things which in themselves have nothing/on themselves.
They are laundered through a set-of-sets logic
shrinking, except they're generative, to a much
smaller world than the world. But an empty word is never
as postponed as money. They don't give you the past,
they offer you —
the fractal present, a bottomless webbing
much deeper than the shallow killing fields of the past.

The found-poem present founders on the past.
Never from a real third person point of view do we see
our *impressive* ship
grind into the crushed hope on the crushing rocks.
We hear about it
in the horribly amplified hull in an artful heartfelt way —
"over!" — to the heartless begging.

Through the dry rib of the ship we imagine a spur
on the outside chance —
ribbed into enough presence of mind — "crooked wood" shedding , germane echo etc. — never to converge
beyond the absent point of perception.])

Not 'wine-dark' but the predisposition is catchy. Caught
with 'wine-dark' in the crime zone (echoing myself
in "Props"). The ruddy rut rattles your brains. You feel Purdy
good when the impounded carpenter screws up your countersunk feelings. 'Intertext' is a synchronous virus,
whiney but not very sloe, I mean dark.

Shifty McLuhan
caught in the clutches of the medium with a thousand voices
geared up for the extended whirlwind tour
barely dutifully able to put things down in order
"to put things down".

Naked again after genealogy,
try on anything.

I keep turning purgatory
— inside-out.

Again my gross dog
nets me "bona fido".

Dr. Johnson bites barkly with his refoot
no worse than a woof in itself giving no ground.

Kant and his vicious circles leave the turbulent air
harder than ever, figuring wildly.

Everything I do subtends symbols,
my dog buries them in the dry salvages
of her solved equations. With my math machine
I dig them up again.
I *work* like a dog though friend
to Aristotle at whom I yell

"Aris, Eros, stetson attractor", which hangs there
with momentum in the unclassifieds

so I say like, demoted and demoted
to salutations

to the oxen butterfly golden axis
of a Hell's Angel's rheumy saliva in the passive wind
that smacked my leg on a hog once.

Without thinking I waved at a horse
yesterday.

Yesterday is about as coloured
yellow
for hurtful ease
as horsepower is made bled to drink.

I like Ike for his military industrial complex comment
(before *JFK*). I like reading because you tear a book apart
ashes to ashes, reforestate your aftertaste.

Writing a book is like giving birth
but to a wrong species usually too big for your —
to hell it rectum.

He wrote quite a few big books, you figure his mind
is a disappearing but hand-tipped synecdoche.

He couldn't dream
because of the cat scanning the pillow
full of little brittle backbones not feathers.

The upper and lower limit
for qualifying for farm assistance actually crossed
yet the papers announced 30 million available.
Here was a case the red tape had Franz in high places.
Franz was a butterfly that came out perfectly crunched
numbers. All the nets were as chaos. A Li Po of faith
and Franz brushed *out* the crotch
like an old Dennis Burton "listening to the [unstoned] stones"
menstruating supernova between the horns of the moon.

The city up to this point had thought
farmers a narcissistic feedlot.
After each went through each's looking glass
you couldn't use that metaphor "seed corn"
because the de-invaginating gyre recalled itself.
Nobody remembered the fertile crescent
when just a twinkle.

Sometime I'd like to do something on Einstein
going chalk mad waxing twinkle.

Cute Girdle looking down on the astrophysicist
as a garage mechanic, but
drinking in Leibniz's unchanging concepts.

"Is that what eventually happens to all physicists?"
"No, only geniuses go mad, you're just going to get dumber
and dumber." Quoted that, of one physicist to another
as they listened to elderly Eddington, to Jon last August,
Jon's last August and he laughed
with gusto.

She and me met in the Zoo (not caught in the metrical rose)
for old time's sake when I'd been wrong
in a way that talking about it now in any mode
would only Gödel it.

"There are some things you can't apologize for"
said Nietzsche's head
on Lou Salomé's forgiving platter, unsaid Nietzsche's warts
thrown in, thrown as
unmastering master, mastered
by the selfless other getting the last *super*.

She spoke of genetics, viruses and immunology
beyond the PhD level (she was always older
even when ten years younger) till I had to smile
not as the mechanism it might have seemed
but because I was dazzled and wanted to put my back
into the sun or sit down and watch an array
of dolphins. Poetry envies science
under certain conditions.

Later she said sex among some kind
of tiny and skinny monkeys
was strickly Dr. Jekel no mister nice guy Hyde this time.

Then, that a leopard was a very cool dude,
it didn't take a genus to see it either.

Borrowing from *Women, Fire and Dangerous Things*
I'd say cladists and pheneticists and Stephen Jay Gouldists
cross and disappear in their own folklore
of scientifically correct choice.

I was trying to get out of the sun by getting into it.
I'm a raggedy Ann lion with a fox for a stole.

The answer to the crossword clue 'Gutenberg'
is as in 'Steve Gutenberg'.
I was wrong, more like Walter Ong.
Mclue's puzzling, Mclue said, was a "big net".

Another fish gets away. Schools dart up
schools dart down schools never get out of school.

"About that long", I spread my arms beyond obtuse.
The gyre is acute despite me. "The lyric ending"

you can't avoid, quoth the Raven,
my non-secretary.

Too many lovers could conceivably
block your free passage unless they meant nothing.

Two enlightenments collide
at "meant nothing".

"I haven't got a publisher for this yet" —
swirl into a splitting ear till everything goes silent
in the House of Escher
liberated by the disagreements of the multi-mediated
calendars
in the kitchen *Lebensraum* of the puppeteer
who came in from the standing army of immediate heat.

Jujubes allowed to stick in my teeth
halfway through a *Globe and Mail* letter.

I looked at her muscular calves again
pumped up
and thought Margaret Visser!

In *Saturday Night*
and one of her many gopher hole articles.
All her connections are meant
to undermine our initial ones, that is to say the ones
that loom in the air, not handed down but around.

If I deduce where the skinned tennis ball is in the dark
and cold rain
from remembering what the dog does and where she goes
when the neighbour slides the old never-painted garage door
open,

and pull it out of the tall grass
in the corner of the wire fence
with freezing hand, and the dog leaps there at it,
I guess we'd say she thinks I'm for all the world
just a better gofer with an 'f', by a nose.

Calves recall themselves in a new fashioned honour
of figurative hourglass
overturning the female meta-figure,
invaginating figures through the crunch of subscripted,
so-called universes. In Lethbridge as a kid with comic books
Dennis Burton learned to draw handguns from a German POW
from a there not exactly
there. The CIA invaginates
superscripturally according to the top secret, namely
that at bottom blind spots see best
and where ideology reduces to the weakest link,
file on! Moment of everybody's birthday,
in the repeat-after sense.

Big ideas via a leverage metaphoric,
or metafork, can perform
hypo dainty creation perceptions.

Where's Margaret Visser when we need her, drag her
so all falls down, netly, neatly falling

through.

By a nose ye shall know me
more
despite me.

Get this: snow on August the 21st! Best potential harvest
ever, though would have been/will be late.
Crops still very green, how much damage and whether
they will stand up again, I don't know. Snow melting today
but continuing. Huge elm branches broken off,
in the driveway. In country in a country

where the seasons are so definite
I called them mutual windshield wipers once. Emotions tied
to seasonal work go dormant as the seasons stretch out, come
to life in cross reference, or quest conch'd in.
"The summer, the unimaginable / Zero summer."
Niet. return. Proust roost. Odysseus'
"transitory [Bloom]/of snow". Zero pre-Laurentian sync-ing,
not kitsch-sinking, *nostos* — well, a quantum of nostalgia
with the Ulysses-pinching *Ulysses* name of the pain —
do well spark-up — cross-fuse.

With everything planted so late
the plan was to spend a short fall summer in Banff
forgetting and gearing up for a load of swathing.
Stick some philosophy lectures into the Xmas present
Walkman. Work while I work, grain against grain.

The pleasure of, not pushing back the frontier,
but of going to seed upstream through systemic inches,
the crushing weight of maso-machismo — hands full
nelson-like
with a barbell across my own neck
and the dog gives me a "Chinese", racist-erased-but-tracist-
raised-&-crossed-in, ie a rubbing haircut on the knee cap
with a slurpy, unabashed pudendum pink tongue.
What counts for sex, letting
the question mark pass like the awkward starving
pricks in the heart, quivering bristles on the knee
out at the knee, untimely quicker-than-quickie
and heavier than lead poisoning in turtle time
to the observing bullet.

One big snowfall at the end of October
last year and then the mildest, dryest winter.
We turned off the kidney machines
for the time it takes to say "Clint East[coker]wood"
and then ran all ski season
for the instant Hollywood town near Calgary.

I have mixed emotions
about the flattened green crops.
The snow has constitutively abused
the structure of time. The injured false knee
sorts out a completely unwanted
sloe gin heeling, keeping the leash limp
and the brown mantle on Shackleton's
Antarctica.

The just last super-imposition
of the waste.

LINEBACKER

There seemed to be a fashion a few years ago
to talk about negative capability. I first realized this
in a Woody Allen movie. Sometime in the seventies
in the Grizzly House in Banff I gave inspired, drunken supple-
mentalry definitions of it to Jon who wrote them down
on a napkin. My brother who was travelling through from SFU
said I was giving away good ideas. But I was capable I said.
Sheila Watson told us how Keats felt he was posthumous
when alive. So you've got your dia-chronic in there. I'm
trying to talk campy colloquial but I'm reminded of looking
into and down on a life you might like to live, like the pit
or whatever they called it in football training before the final
cuts where, as a linebacker, you had to take on a firing-out
guard and a charging fullback. As a token fullback they used
their allstar. The guard was MVP of the league. As a Tolkien
linebacker they used me. Having a big centre and quarterback
there made it an intimidating four against one. One time

I was late for practice because I got engrossed in the teach-
in wherein Ernest Manning debated a philosophy professor.
I told one of the coaches who was an ex-Eskimo why
I was late. He yelled he didn't care if Jesus Christ was
at Convocation Hall. I was the centre for a drill testing
various defences. A corruptible sentence but not me and not
in the sense of "too far gone"! I had worked up quite a sweat
but was getting a bit of a chill bent over with those tight
football pants in the crisp fall evening while the coach,
the atheist become quarterback, kept putting his hands
into position and then thinking of another point to make
to the defense. One point followed another as he absent-mind-
edly kept flicking his hands into position and then thought
of something more to say. Well the upshot was it was getting
quite ticklish so I kept standing up which made me appear to be

slacking off and besides I was in his way as he instructed
the defensive tackles etc. So he would push me down again.

The night after we lost the first Save the Children College
Bowl, 14 to 7 to the Toronto Varsity Blues, we partied
pretty seriously in the Royal York Hotel. An alumni player's
cousin and her girl friend who were both from Toronto
were up in the rooms and "slept" with half the team
was the rumour. Somebody walked into the bathroom
on the cousin who had her back to the open door as she bent
down and looked at him upside down from between her legs,
pantiless bum etc. The way I was told this and with my-my
own position, not as centre (and middle guard), actually
wandering, as well as with the passage of time, I re/
member it as if I had been the one who had walked in/on her.
This is probably how the imagination appropriates religious
experience. Though I remember the cousin's girl friend giving

me a big kiss once. I had been self-conscious about my wispy
mustache. This was before the CFL allowed players to have
beards. When hippies were a threat. On the one hand
I published erotic poems in the campus literary magazine
and on the other, played football. Up the middle I was skipping
classes and flunking out. On my calculus exam I wrote
it's been a trying year yet with not too much trying. I forget
what I wrote on the modern abstract algebra and didn't
even go to the physics. To miss a physics lab was major
and the first one I missed was an experiment in itself, lying
there on my bed when it was late but not too late to catch up,
then borderline and then definitely too late.
The chemistry of it!

One night in the dark but for the lights
from the phys. ed. building we were huddled around the coach
with his clipboard. This was a final practice and then sermon
before we flew to Toronto. My beard stuck out from under
my face guard and cast a shadow on the clipboard.
In the middle of the sermon the coach looked at me

with a sharp eye and said the beard went — not to Toronto.
I took advantage of this situation to let my mustache catch
up with my beard — bad reasoning. Pathetic white wispy
mustache. One of the two stewardesses that came up
to the Royal York too, said she didn't like my mustache on me.
I guess I can think I could have thought of the cousin
of the Wife of Bath and now true through Magritte
and the unthought master the Mona Lisa, then back stage
to a movie, made-in Madonna, full circle to the cousin again.

Immaculate anything — say epicycles or upward spirals,
vertiginous virgins (all necessary evils given all
the down-to-earth grace, and bottom-up going over/halfway
so getting extremely implicated in the monopolar rolling
with the punches' indices — holes up in everything,
ie not so Judo disorientedly full moebius as to be up on top
of going down, though this is a suspicious pulling of the irony
which irony, incidentally, defies either of the tidy monopoles
especially the one where the extensional mess promotes itself
unintentionally as intensional message — as it were, ingrained
grains of sand Liebniz-pregnant all over again. Everything
bigger and smaller at the same time through the backdoor or
vul-gate, O unimbibed bibil-us, up pop/pin'!
Anything immaculate *draws in* a mess, marking it
with "whatever comes to what". A mess is clean up to
not-itself, messiah within sin. The miracle of the hollow men
is staggered on the sinking-in superficies. Raw/cooked
mustache annihilated to a choice draw — ex nihilo right into
the gist in erased gestation, actually absorbed into
the displaced weight of a face insinuated to a bleeding edge
always already placing itself, like Einstein's vampire mirror
ahead of the light, so relatively prior to itself, and going
steady with the ex/panding universe. The arrow of time
is only a close shave looking back. All sentences are indented
and, that one especially, wrinkled.

Before the topic of whiskers, actually outside of this account,
re-emerging from reading Peirce's account of his struggle
with nominalism and then just now reading Noel Annan's
Our Age, I was reminded of Occam's razor and how
it's beginning to apply to me in the last six weeks
since January. Cut to the quick / anecdotes is not enough
though Burroughs' cutups are corrective enough.
Notice the equivocal spread between the 'enough's.
That's interest that favours neither the lender nor the borrower and is why Burroughs begs the question with which
Peirce finally pierced the nominalists' point, which moved
him closer to Hegel. If you're going to use cutups one way not
to overlook trying would be not the method but the intelligence, re agency, to leave the razor in the text. Not
the slightly bleeding face which is as embarrassing in a small
objectifying mode — which in the face is irreconcilable —
as a premature mustache which, though self-conscious, is not
at all the same as the mustaches of women. Things change
of course over time.

I missed my girl friend that weekend in Toronto. That was
the year we broke up. We kept breaking up for many years
after. In fact there were more years breaking up than years
of core relationship. When some of the reviewers of *Banff/
Breaking* implied it had a moralistic streak
and admonished that breaking also had positives
I was annoyed, because I knew that. I mean there are almost
too many semantic-blended-to-usage equivocations
in the choppy water text. From breaking the ice to breaking
wind, while the sections break the points of view
and narratives of one another, notwithstanding new fusings.
Also the pretending-to-greater-perspective sections break
into neutral oblivion rather than omniscience. However
the most sustained narrative, cut up, but reseeded chronologically, is, admittedly, sentimental. Regardless
breaking up is liberating, a participle that needs
to participate on the other side, to involve

an "object", reconstituted beyond anybody's pleasure. More
dialectic here than meets the eye. Gramarye. The beginning
of the incurable chatting up rules. See Ford Madox Ford
on talk sex talk, where the pretext root carries not the day
but the talk and the talk intransitively cures, like hay say.
Jazz transcendental: the talk is the sex and the sex is
the phone and all the phone is had.

I wandered around the hotel a lot. The reason we lost was
not because we were the poorer team but because it was
a mud bowl and their line outweighed ours by, on average,
ten pounds. Our vital passing attack was nullified
by the Toronto mud not the Blues. Anyway I didn't play.
I watched the Winnipeg Rods who were staying on
the same floor, standing around the elevator area
in their suits and top coats looking askance at the orgy
evolving from room to room-ance — in the pants.
The "cousin" came flying around the corner (I remember seeing
this) and jumped on the upright coach (three points for split-
ting the 'upright's just this instant replay converted
as the meaning started taking), arms around his neck, legs
around his waist. The three points?: his crossbar Catholicism,
her doing downright goal posts.

The night before the game a defensive half, who went
from 165 to 185 pounds the next summer on steroids, and I
took advantage of free tickets and went to *King Rat*
and then Maple Leaf Gardens where from as far up
and as far back as you could get and three deep, by jumping,
I saw Bobby Hull fly around the rink. Well he wasn't that fast,
I jump-cut more than once. I had been a Mahovlich fan
but was going off him then and Hull was in the process
of transmigrating to "Bobby Clobber". Coming out
of the Gardens onto the street we saw a car skid and slam
into the car in front, right in front of us, intersectionwise.
Toronto was fairly overwhelming for an O Mitchell kid
from the prairies. Actually that first sense of "history"
(Arendtian depth), which is the word we use for a certain

palpable feeling, occurred to me somewhere after
the cobblestones in the rain and sort of during the walk
by a wrought iron fence, looking at what I recall as the Edin-
burgh-like sooted masonry of the U of T buildings
and, cornball enough (stuff of eternity, perish the thought),
names and dates chiselled into the stone.

Eventually the Winnipeg Rods began loosening their ties
and putting their top coats over their arms. They had looked
the real football players, heads back, neck-conscious
as they swelled them out of their stiff white collars.
I did that I know even though it seemed you got away with it
because you were just trapped, with a swollen neck.
And you were because you didn't know any better. The Rods
were the last guys to go to bed, sometime after six. They lost
the next day Sunday, 58 to nothing or something, the national
championship, after waking with the cousin and her teammate.

I flew with the band and the injured players in a prop plane.
The next year that I was back at university ('67)
after becoming sure-fire for first string
I was secretly relieved when told I couldn't play
because I'd flunked a year. Out of nowhere "I bought the farm"
— full speed game unsituation pun, or half speed:
I bought the farm and then flipped it into the subjunctive
imaginary, road to glory hell paved with no intention,
astro-turfing the iron grid. Burning desire.
Then a mountain meadow with tender little shoots.

Gone for broke and coming out ahead in kind
on the other, Ararat Titanic, with full knowledge and with no
now need of it. On the Hemingway tip taking the Lemming way
flip, an ocean back, liner trip. Disease runs its course
into the hour glass ocean where the notion of totality is inter
-rupted by another interrupted totality and so on breeding
more lemmas and a logical world of incompleteness
that takes off the designs on the earth-world.
Each lemming crowds out the Canetti laws, sweeps

the ice for the curling un-enKroetsching spa novel.
To mention the Battles of Lemberg would be too encyclopedic!

All *totalled*, a lot of liberational breakage: romantic,
educational and then the rut of sports. The moments
of alienation that know what's good
for your prepossessed self
and know how to preserve themselves in the world
made *over*, and hoping to start again or for the first time
they can seem so long — these master moments.

We stopped down in Winnipeg to refuel after the long hours
in the air, but it was so foggy the band got out
its instruments and started marching around the then
new terminal until they finally put us up in the Fort Garry
Hotel and gave us a big banquet room to amuse ourselves in.
I'd never felt much belonging on the football team, really
brought home when I stepped on a big frat rat tackle's toes
with my cleats in another general huddle around the coach.
Not the look but the tone of the growl! And yet the band
were so artsy I didn't have much in common with them either.
Felt close to the steroid kid and the guy with a name
like 'Nesterenko' who had a huge cast on one leg
and was also a basketball player. No sticking-out intended
sticking in 'Nesterenko' in the Anglo-centric-present-
ation-of-strange-name cliché
(hyphenation stat-us irony intended), except in the ironic truth
that it isn't forgotten as completely as a what's-in-a-spear
'Shaftesbury' say. It *is* recalled in fact
but the velleity of its answering is blocked
in a protect-the-innocent feint. Nesterenko of course,
like lichen, was hock / eye's Black Hawk nemesis
shadowing Mahovlich like a dirty dreamwork, worst nightmare
freely associating. Strange things will happen under
the midnight sun. In the beginning

when radio football first received me in a Grey Cup / area,
for all practical purposes, I knew the Edmonton Eskimo

Jackie Parker as Jackie "Parka", and the image worked
even as it was itself hooded, just as 'Eskimos's
leading out of a gypped people, gyps itself,
till wild fans, rooting for the cause / of hysteria,
perpetually reorder the name for itself,
just as leaping blind loyalty switches the body's place
in itself. Gyprock ears on the Statue of Liberty fake.
Gypsies caught between being caught and the arrest of same.

That 'Parker' had been bent into 'Parka', unwitting imaginary
crossing of the public language barrier,
complete with a proto-anthropology or half-built dreams
of a unified field, blind-siding back and warping
the public world without trace, like the adjusted-out
of-the-light-speed-picture speed of the light source —
if you publicize your invisibility the public world insinuates,
not itself into the private world, it just insinuates
not-itselfness, as the site of imaginary ownership clashes
which of course are collapsible to actual private bodies
that are headed for actual black holes, both terminable
worm and interminable worm hole,
springing the pockets inside out again,
but the most shrunken clashing imaginary is actual
and infinitely restitutional, ie there is always a moment
where the baddest thing — the "hypercorrect" child phrase

is only hope sizing up — is as feckless as my 'Parka'
with no exterior, the consolation being
not in the (so far) baddest thing, restitutionally subsumed,
but in the unheld centri/fugal clash — that 'Parker'

had been bent into 'Parka' (an image of him
doing a jump pass with the ball like a hood behind his head,
insisted darkest before the dawn), broke in upon me, mock —
like the persistent news of Newton's light
upon refractory Goethe as he built plants up out of leaves
(almost *t-s* 'd out "plan" [*t* leaves another clued-in circle]),
even as his leaves were the brilliant [a]head-of-their-time

cells obscured, not by their being bud-closed
but by the very openness of their own undivided suggestion —

mocked 'Parker', mocked me,
at the Drumheller swimming pool playing football
on the surrounding grass with the for-the-summer friend
who put the feeling-small fear of Drumheller into me
with his wintry correction. I was with my older cousin,
a champion swimmer then and still a musician
who hears only Beethoven on an exceptionally scratchy record.
Her parents in an extended family
joke used 'gouge' for 'gorge'. She was old enough to be full
of sounded worlds when eardrumheller struck again
in a dislocation. She ate her word just as quarterbacks
the balls, family resemblance chews out the home
away from home, game. Ringo the lingo.

When I think of the huge paintings in that banquet room
I can't see the content, sort of project the picture
of a buffalo herd in our basement (a dangling "hohoho" till it
folds) and the huge painting with real bullet holes
from the American Civil War in Drumheller in the house
of the people from Georgia who lived right
beside Mrs. Drumheller. Or was it Mrs. Drumheller's house?
This is not a real time question, not even with real time
modesty, sub-lated, then again, the fake performer time
is done to your perfect enough undoing in real time.
You in 'your' are both undone and doing the undoing of me.
All is not lost in this pro-leapt-tick of fake faith.
Neither is paradise a crackdown on the gulflessness of real
time, just as real time is cracked up to be what it's not.

I'm taking a break right now, going for a coffee at the Cake
Company in Banff and read the *Globe and Mail*, Rick Salutin's
fifth column (March 6/92 — the CBC *Sunday Report*
in its rest/rictive electronic idea of a town hall meeting).
The supermarket is playing one of those games
where they try to get you to try a new variation-on-a-theme

product by withholding the original. This will be the third
day. Autobiography is like the essentiality of the body
in perception. But of course there are big problems
with essentiality. Right here the most Merleau-Ponty
incarnated I could go, as fluctuated holi medium macro
and abducted into the existentially symbolizing graphs
on the super page, would be to whole-sell out
and to allude to say, Lyn Hyjinian, ie that I've read her
My Life, as my hone/sty. The centre not so much doesn't hold
but rather beholds so much, out the other side.
Hence the curious Poundian minted-ness and synchronous
embedded-in-amber removedness. The rhetoric of honesty,
the honesty of rhetoric, the laser Lazarus Greek-
into-Christian logos, word made flesh made word,
unre/deemed, beams up and stops, punch pulled against punch
drunk. You can think without "language" but not without signs
and then language attracts all signs, strangely.

Months later in this very line I'm trying to remember
whether (with s'pports)
the above stanza was written before I went for coffee.
To be honest I think it was, so to be honest
in the first place, only having per- and pre-used the Salutin
column. I was thinking in this new present, but a while ago,
of calling the collection — in which dog pile this "[Talkin']
Linebacker" has not lost its ground nerves
but gained some gangliated agains — "Wrinkle Wall Rhetoric",
the *curious* metaphor coming from the slicks
used (pre-used? re appearances re treads) on dragsters,
the surfaces "given" to backward, self-touching confront-
ations. Friction is stranger when it doesn't break loose
but draws on the all-at-once illusion of age informing,
building up stress and miss-peaking itself, never arriving
in time, mind suddenly sunk in, then lost in pointed-out ways.

Fred James went to the Calgary Stampeders and Ed Molestad
(down the road a lawyer who — recapping over serial
drunken driving charges — defended an Edmonton Oiler),

went to the Eskimos I *Knows Best* when Getty *understood* "Spaghetti Legs". In a *Saturday Night* article a few years ago about the old boy network Getty recounted rooming around with Parker who was on some strong medication. They'd both gotten into their beds and realized they'd left the light on. Getty offered to get up but 'Legs said he would just float up and unscrew the bulb. The hone sty here hides the uptopian function buried in the political rhetorics that are relentlessly reflexive but never admit to screwing with the light spiral. This is not the portentous ending Tom Wayman in an acronym proscribed. Nor is it the unconscious textual narcissism that slyly serves up a metaphor to conclude authoritatively on in a naturalistic "unauthored", *a fortiori* authoritative way. It occurred to me listening to P.K. Page on the radio when she confessed how she couldn't understand how authors could get so egotistical about what were essentially gifts that a new egotism had emerged: to be who is given, to gifts

— K. Burke emerging from Nietzsche with unstoppable goodness waves going through them like so-long neutrinos. On Geez-us' other hand goodness is you aiming into the afterlife for practical purposes. You don't ever want to become yourself, in respect to your joke death but also, with respect, you don't want to be seen appearing, because con-sequential good's necessary ownership suffers the arch-split t/here. A bridging intention is the farce of the splitting one, human in the initial ma/ma way and all too human the other da/da way back, ie empty because fulfilled of itself, where the free particular origin of the stretch mark is "Jack-Deemed" back into the prelapsarian fold.

To be ek-split-it, you don't want to be seen looking good, becombing or becombining yourself, then you're no better than a neutrino jumping around in the shower to get wet, good and wet. But of course a neutrino is always too good ever to get wet. Your good aim can be "diverted" in the mean

time though in Guy Debord's sense of quoting yourself
even when it's Kierkegaard you're quoting. Like a local ir-
rigation project, not changing rivers like a bad metaphor.
But even here you never get wet

                because the good metaphor carries your tuning
into the beyond where you never arrive, just a little bit crazy
getting halvier and halvier in the half lives,
whereas *fin*/essing the tactical monism into the have-not
Eleatic geography of the aesthetic projection,
the practical critique blows up the neutrino as big as a cake
that puts the real/theoretical particle to shame,
another reason it's so hard to be good, belittling others
like this, and laughing at the cosmic cause
sticking to its effects ("the little Egyptian bump" buy-out,
an imaginary equal and opposite exposed to the lever-age
of the light of the temporary assymmetry of time —
the time of late capitalist warriors, or of the peace dividend
divided and demeaned by privation the private Cam-
bridge-drawing Apostle, able Keynes, seeks in the con-quest
of the consequences, in the effect-cum-a-cause pie lot,
ie the economic "peace" between the wars?), laughing
at the stinky big bang blowing without effect
at the rebel angles of the dead candles
in Plato's general *mise-en-abyme* beam trans/former.

Re the big bang-signed stink: the killing, with kindness, irony
is that its stink, itself, doesn't stink,
re the k-nows despite the nose, unless you want to regress
to those halvier half lives. To gauge this disengagement
it must be said that the tripartite topologies in Plato's poetic
capture and forget more empirical labour,
albeit either hyper- or hypo-human, than the great pyramids.
(Human tragedy occurs in that, this tiny but elastic gap
through hyper and hypo.) Re "good while you're sleeping":
ask a contemporary distance runner if she can't get into Zeno,
even locked into, but then that's Zeno with opposite spin.

I look at my watch: 8:14, about right, letting fly
my smart, secondhand apperception.

Ed Molestad was about 6′ 8″ or at least 6′ 5″.
Many years later I recognized him in Banff
in my friend's restaurant. He'd put on more weight
and was putting on some more. With his lankiness it was hard
to realize how muscularly large he was when he was lean.
In a two arm shiver drill his hand must have slipped off
my shoulder pad so to hit and break off my tooth. I never felt
a thing until a few minutes later my tongue felt the strange
gap. Recurringly I'll dream that tooth is trying to break out
of my mouth, the pressure is unbearable and it seems
like the cap has reached its limit, will break off too,
and then I wake up. I guess that's a body memory of no
consequence or a nerve impulse that got screened in
and doted on by a one note, dystopian speculation, a unit
of hysteria locked into memory. A couple of years ago
our new Labrador jumped up on me late at night
after I'd come home from the farm and chipped another tooth
with her teeth. Through the mirror for an instant — long in
the tooth, even clod — recap. Slightly sad with the thought behind
how it didn't really matter. Middle age resignation.
But a relieved maturity too. And the impulse bent back
into the irresistable exuberance of the dog.

The dentist who put the cap on
called over a young woman with a beautiful smile
to look in my mouth at my teeth. What is that thing
that hangs down at the back of your mouth like a fleshy tooth,
not a tonsil? The next week I recognized
the new beauty queen on the front page of the Gateway
as the dental assistant.

In Sheila Watson's English class I sat beside a powerful phys.
ed. student who cast aspersions at Sheila and yet
was very friendly to me. I gave him considerable recognition,
considering. Sheila told me after class once not to get caught

between two stools, meaning physics and English.
Jon told her I was quite big years later — the telling and,
Jon-unwittingly, some of the bigness, later,
well all of the bigness as a relative difference
as far as Jon could be telling. He said she told him
she didn't remember that part but rather remembered a flame
at the back of the room, and her, a "tiny" woman
trying to get tinier, all too aware of the pirate cross
sermo[u]n[t]ing the right hand *who* begeth big. For quite
a while the phys. ed. guy and I sat at the very front.
I thought Jon was reporting my nervousness to me
but later thought he meant she meant the colour of my hair.
Anyway it was no doubt a speechless flame. A geist
with zits. Maybe Jon ignited the image of the phys. ed. guy
in her when she checked for big.

Sheila quite often lost everybody with extensive flights
of explanation. She told me I used her essay topics as
runways. I wrote her a poem with the image
of my mother's cocker spaniel, dead before I was born,
picking up marbles from the floor until he reached the point
they would start falling out. Or till someone squeezed him
just inside the top of his back legs. Then all the marbles
came out. They called that dumping him and took turns,
or probably fought for them. The anecdote had wanted to be
an allegory — rather I had wanted it to be,
which makes all the difference because an allegory is
an allegory because *it* wants to be. The saturation story
was too short, straight and knotless or not enough
a nautilus — or W.C. Williams machine? (see Fields below) —
too simply dumped to be an economizing allegory.

And now I want through this not-allegory an allegory
of allegory where the dogmaw tries to gobble up all
the smarts in the purlieu
and through an anti-unrecuperative move on its part,
supplant itself with a hegemonic move on the parts
of the purlieu. The active/passive flip out of "the parts"

in the grammar retrodicts the undecidability of the justness
of the hegemonized decided.

Or the dogmaw opens and loses all its marbles shouting
"shoot the dog, shoot the dog!",
that punchline in *Alice Doesn't Live Here Anymore*
that points to the pointless, throws everybody off just
for the hell of it. The only telltale sign that the dogmaw —
chasing its allegory — hasn't shot the rabids
of itself is the dry retro rhetor drool of the prophet,
his uncrossed hell hauteur.

Allegory that really goes through the motions, tricks itself
out to chance, intimates a second — the all-embracing little
later — the silent "come" — creating the subtle strength
                                  of a field
into which three times the voice is thrown: first because
it already is, second because it already *as* — dogmaw's
fetching mask, third as "blasted allegory",
the ploughing of prophets back where words *in* -appropriate
copies of buried masters, keep
exploding Shakespeared characters
with something like *strength* of character emanating a-cross
ghost writers' fiction fields that influence the all-too-ex-
pressed good soldiers. Fields never themselves wholly
selves or wholly impressed, kicking children, kicking dogs,
the life and death habit, getting a kick out of
the larger than life — the per*pet*ual at large.
                        Big Daddy Freud Sig-mundi-o admits
"wild analysis" will work despite itself
as it d[e]rives the patient back to her own derivations,
"who" know no transcendental signifido — but bay
at the marble-less dogmaw, obey the marble-us field.

Wilfred took over her class one day and caught my attention
by reversing field, getting very intensive about metaphor.
This was around the time Wilfred must have been working
with McLuhan on *From Cliche to Archetype*

that everybody said but for a few flashes of brilliance
was unreadable. I loved it. Reading McLuhan's letters
and then Marchand's biography it was interesting to find out
how scattered they were doing the book
and how difficult it was being a co-author with McLuhan.
Sheila enjoyed the cultural life when they lived in Toronto.
McLuhan's old carriage house communications centre
I imagined not better but more inevitably after driving around
the campus and going to the bookstore in the old library in '88.
Carried Toronto '88, somewhere around the Bud McDougal/
Conrad Black house, into *Self-Condemned* I only read about
'90. "That of course should have been London, Ont."
is what I wrote in an earlier draft. London should of course
be Windsor where Lewis actually lived, as well as in Toronto
" . . . that I'm sure I was aware of at the time of reading"
I continued and continue with no quotation marks now,
real time deficit. Performative cop out! Or inevitable,
rootless platonic passion reified into police / place lines?
Yet isn't performative supposed to be so all consuming
authentic? Another naturalistic collapse! Good strategy
though. Thomistic radiance off the backhand.
And yet unapperceptively a dark horse or house did buy out
the heart of *Self-Condemned.*

Chris Dewdney said in Lethbridge he found England
oppressive. I assumed more palpabilities, many times over,
of what I liked that disoriented time in the rain, football-
embarrassed, the clearing onto sooted cobblestones — in short
that too much of a sense of history possessed him. Funny if
you think the further twist of eons of geological time he
revels in. Not so funny of course either.

The pit of my stomach is with me I noticed a few days ago
when I was on a live radio broadcast from the Banff Springs
Hotel. What a lovely wet snowy morning, early Sunday
morning — after the show! The pit of my stomach
was with me in the pit of firing-out guard
and charging fullback. Negative capability is inevitable

perhaps especially when you go into the pit. Living as
they say in the belly of the beast it's hard to identify the pit.
Is it big guts or little guts? Not exactly
Hegel's idea of sacrifice you don't mind committing
if you've found the perpendicular front, or exterior blast.
The pit of the stomach, the belly of the beast. I think again
of Archie J. Baum's Chinese mediation between Western will-
fulness and India's will-lessness: willingness, which absorbs
duty *and* pleasure, like constituent particles.
Everything's on the table here including the naturalistic fall-
acy. Unlike "the pit", physics is carried over to the boundary
where metaphorology is minimized and metaphoricity falls
into "originary catacreshtic violence." Otherwise
I have to invoke Martin Buber and his being prey to God,
to end on an après-John-Donne pun.

One more anecdote whose scene is re-called Lister Hall
on the Edmonton campus. The place was primarily
a huge cafeteria but there were lounges downstairs
where couples would neck until student patrols
would interrupt them. Funny how the point of view here,
coming to it over these years, is now closer to the patrol
side, less unwillingly so, too, than the original patrollers,
taking into account their twisted self-repressive pleasure.

One couple went up to the usually empty, large foyer in back
of the cafeteria. They chose the least lit area to sit
on a bench, and under their coats did the best they could
with their "physically challenged" passion. They were both
from farms but hardly considered themselves jerky peasants
until about five young men filed out of the double doors
with an obvious eye gap opposite the bench. Each had a smirk
on his face. The couple had been more desperate than daring.
At least the men didn't applaud and the lovers didn't reach
irritably after any fact or reason.

The Energy of Slaves — I liked the title better than the book.
Probably time to take another look. I would whimsically like

to say they walked across the downs in April rain after some
terrible trial endured, so that the cold wet weather was balm
to their dilated vessels, niacin high now, and in overproof-
rock England, the four quartzes or something.

In the pale indirect light of predawn at the back of Lister
Hall, in front of the Men's residence, whose two wings were
like thighs, sixties thighs, and welcoming arms in tandem,
a gymnast commerce student's bellows drifted up
all ten stories into the breathing windows. I looked out
from the sixth floor, the quiet guy from across the hall
who could walk on his hands all the way to the bathroom
and even open the swing door. I never looked to see if
into the urinal he could piss upside-down
and kind of backward. There he was, head tilted back, drunk
as a skunk, bellering from wing to wing.
With his hands he sculpted and wanked a huge, imaginary
cannon of a cock. He was like a village fire siren that had to
run its course — on and on he went, wanked.
Finally we heard him through two doors, get off the elevator,
then roaring down our hallway, "I don't play favourites,
I knock on this door and I knock on this door!" Already
colonized by the cad/ence (*Only He and me knew and now
only He* was her bit of Eliot lore.), we waited to be born
and Lougheed **bowled**

over, despite ourselves, into wooden alleys, the thundering
before the lightning strike, time-smeared and ambiguated
in the creating of a primal scene cum part scenes,
the vertical disintegrals of the body, sperm men,
the sex comedy of directing and being in
the rites of passage which are both outsized and inadequate
like the lion's roar rented in the escape back in the maw

which touch, never-the-less, the now edge,
everything wonted — tomb-essence, the inhabitation by little
others, shooting messengers, the tomb-innocent phantoms
of all the nerve.

FOOTNOTES

Jon looked perhaps fifty when I saw him at twenty-five,
he looked a healthy fifty when he was fifty finally.

He told me someone said he looked like
a laterally compressed Frank Mahovlich.

Woody Allen a bit of course
and a model one year in a liquor ad.

On June 15th, 1991 I shouted across
two tables in a restaurant in Edmonton
to say he looked like Preston Manning.

Jon had been at a music conference
where Marvin Minsky talked about artificial intelligence,
and had listened in to some Reform Party members
in the faculty club. "Speaking of artificial intelligence"
— the secret, pre/ludic tenor
of Jon's nerve, decentral ear-to-the-ground
poem for voices for sacred rivers.

In the Southern Alberta Art Gallery
I was talking to the curator's husband, a biology professor
at the U of L, and he told me about the biology of strokes
and I told him about Richard Hugo
who drank for the hangovers.
Independently I knew the experience
but also heard a medical man
say liquor was initially a depressant
and as it wore off, a stimulant.

I told him about the time
Ernest Manning was lured to Convocation Hall
in Edmonton for a debate. A young philosophy professor
syllogistically established that Manning thought
of himself as truly inspired and was therefore
a dangerous crackpot.

Eli Mandel got up at this point
shaking and very red in the face, "what about Yeats?!"
he shouted, howled and Halled out other poets.

But Ernest didn't need help, even inadvertant help,
proceeding to mop the floor with the attacker
and the questioners from the floor
which greatly confused us. Finally he stood up
in his three piece suit and very shiny shoes I remember,
looked at his watch and said he really should be going.

Nobody had any more ammunition and the syllogism
which wasn't even the so-called practical syllogism
ended with a whimper.

Manning the door of the syllogism
everything drifted into a dangling gender
Eli whipped once before the drift kind of got to us

but which Ernest maddeningly topologized
into the separation of church and humour.

He had told the shaggy one about digging a pit
beside the church for the ashes from the wood-burning stove
for the kickline that ended "in the ash-hole."

The other day we were watching the Queen's 40th anniversary
and her role as the Buck [King] *ham*
stops here — standin' joke
you can tell
the avant / Bakh*tin* dance
from the stood up comedian.
The dry line to the Americans the day after

she was dwarfed by microphones
brought down the government
house. The ghost writer had great immaterial
to work with — low Highness.

She's a punchline everyone backs off from
till an elaborate in-joke meets what's ex-spectacled.
The *Globe and Mail* "thought du jour" (August 25/92 —
5 months after the start of this poem) was
"kings are not born; they are made
by artificial hallucination"— the ham G.B. Shaw, bucking
the system till the last shall be first.

Even the smallest consumer choice cuts you
out of the background — makes you
weightless for a moment then second thought as leaves
nose to ground
where the root of opera works and doesn't
as it does.

Persons are only personifications. Antique antics are suited
for an anti-position. No person can fill it
except insofar as others are
"sucked in" by the power vacuum.

The G&M Arts page "Artifact" quote is "Ideas are one thing,
and what happens is another" — John Cage (1912-1992).

Of course the epitome of what happens hemorrhages
in a Queen's hands brief ideas with barely a chance.
In pre-industrial times where bloodlines were in search
of no-joke daring dada
and balls in their court,
held-up data were transfused into monstrous actions.

Generally dramatism reigns though now beyond binarism
and into the digital is it, as they say, full circle retardy time
for chance and charm again?

When John Cage was in Banff Jon had him down
to Catherine's house where he got Jon, without the bp 'h',
turned on to the operation of chance in writing.
We attended his symphony for radios years later.
None of the radios could get any stations,
only static on the mountain.

Jon said Cage looked like Huckleberry Hound and I laughed
at the sudden disharmonious clarity Cage received
just about the time he was getting testy about synaesthesia,
which didn't interest him, in question period.

Couldn't remember the name of the hound so phoned
the bookstore who phoned the library. Phoned my brother
to find out if the snowed-down crops had sprung back at all.
They had, looking pretty good in fact, but the frost (Aug. 24)
he thought had killed them. *Double* blind he wiggled one
antenna of the race: Huckleberry buried in old TV snow
came in crystal clear and on top of that, reached
that extra radiance over and above his being such
a singular flake — my brother's "keeper"!
He used to get all the sports questions too
on *Reach for the Top*. My brother! Mistaken me.

One time I couldn't remember "Van Morrison".
It came up "Donovan" each time until "Donovan Morrison."

Ronald Ray guns return to the sun
what was Caesar said than done.

With a Thatch roof over his head
he brushed up on the Queen's English, a pool term
for playing for shape, so that nothing actually counts
in the cued-up present danger.

There were two coeval Samuel Johnsons, one kicked Berkley,
the other wrote Hume a letter from America
to the effect that causes on billiard tables were one thing
throne into many, but the human agent was something else.

The Ernst *Bloch-ed* principle of hope takes a splintered
Freudian pathology. The intent of the silly-jism split / spilt
from the purloined letter — leaving the unsettled state
of "natural reactions". When Manning left what remained
was everything saved from out-of-time spirit.
Evil is the collapse of categories said Hegel as
he endlessly emerged, from nature for instance
and instant memorization.

My mother's father used to listen to Bible Bill on the radio
and get mad. Grandmother split 'mad' into the sin of anger
and the madcap who switched
on the show.

My father knew Bible Bill as the school teacher in Calgary,
Crescent Heights.

Kroetsch mixed rye and the same radio
in *The Words of My Roaring* .

Sunday sermons turned up in a lot of older American poetry
as it tried to fill the shoes.

My mother's father was an MLA and said Brownlee
was a good man. Jon in his column and Heather Robertson
on *Morningside* implied he was guilty of sexual harassment.

The doctor said my mother's head was "empty", a prescription
we filled à la Descartes, the joke of the collapsed
coordinates on us, on us — our reflex, deficit-soaring spirits!

Every perspective on things begs "a perspective on things".
Ethics and epistemology collapse into one another.
Normativity is born and never falls to "metaphysical realism"
or with the death of any particular normative —
Hilary Put'n'em, the empiricists, in his Put'n'em place,
the necessary re-presentation falling to no choice
but choosing, the acutest impalement of the obtuse beyond.

On the way into the doctor's office
to get the results of my mother's cat scan
the entrail news was on the road-kill radio,
little white crossings dee dumb dee dumb
all over the blacked-out map.
The reporter the newscaster "went to"
told us the American health care system was "sick"
and needed "care". Bush's speech writer gave us,
with parallel competence, some bushit (no 'l' llama)
". . . those who are scribbling out prescriptions for disaster".

Metaphors out of hand,
metaphors collapse two birds.
Concepts are overdetermined
in both senses,
one sense remedies the other, and vice versa.

"Truth is a goal that includes the process of getting there"
— Hegel there. A path is Heidegger's humble way,
everywhere and nowhere is its province as it leads on.

Moody analysts say moody mood-transcendent Heidegger
lead us on all right, "fetishizing Being", big B-ing it etc.
(probably as good as any*thing* to fetishize) and my feeling
was as much as to say so, also, well before the big Nazi
discussion began in the press in North America in about '87.
Now beyond a certain ripe disquiet — I get disgusted
with my own enthusiasms — a ghost moment to the quietest
event still seems in order, always out of order.

After being
"into him" —
circumnavigation
even as the ship's planks impale
hedge's edge — critique creak of age.

Not all my memories are vital signs.
The Invention of Memory is a good book
period for self-prophetic reconstructions. It is not

the means of production anymore but the invisible
means of the demeaning return
of the unrepressed *returns*!

I'm not into string theory but knot theory, strings of knots
are turning into knots but the saving one is the one without
the 'k', the signed letter to the unsound answer in the in-
faux-manic in-tarot-aero-gating castle.
K-tel ads used to wag into oblivion as they tried to back up
your mind even as you got your back up. Hegel said there's no
need to go beyond circumstances which can hold their own.
This is freedom like the switch to writing
between Homer and Plato but not like the empty freedom
of the first half of Sartre
Adorno cites as the other side to committed art
which overplays its hand.

Reading a lot makes you write real big.
Writing a lot makes you read big,
ie consciousness per square inch, or better yet,
bang for your buck, of this last eat the meat
and throw away the bones. Marrow is not the essence
of bones. Peter Van Toorn said "choked on a love fish",
you know what, which is a bit graphic what
with the meta-phorplay delay.

Two bigs have to wait one
for the other, if they try to step into the future
together.

I was standing in the existential as-structure
when the biology professor told me about a brilliant
remittance man who had a drinking problem
unless he lived in the bush
to where people drove miles to hear him talk
and how he wrote daily to his mother in England
brilliant letters which the brother burned
when the mother died.

I forgot to mention the huge "bush" paintings around us
by Stephen Hutchings. They put me in a Thomas Hardy mood.
The catalogue said just as human existence is in limbo
bushes persist in a middle ground of botanical hierarchy.

This is just a rough draft but with enough superim-pose
to smooth move on the future O perfect reader,
gnome de ruffled plumes.

On a personal note, moon-landing tuning-fork irresponse,
we've just had another Caesar salad and whether
it's generic or the way my mother makes it
as soon as I get a forkful of lettuce
and as many croutons as possible up to my mouth
which starts to water, it all falls off.
Maybe that's why I like it so maddeningly much.

This afternoon my mother watched one of the seven videos
for eleven dollars. With the glass den door pulled shut
and the video, and mother not hearing as well,
the young Labrador naturally wanted in. With a kind
of politeness or shyness surprising for this one
being hyper — "they're either hyper or placid" —
but also with a sense of appropriate response
she goes through an astonishing repertoire of yowlings,
whimpers, barks, half-barks etc. What really gets me
is that leathery snapping ear flapping, thinking of her
down there looking through the bevelled glass
and all those spectral colours released, lost on her.

Sometimes that ear flapping is an irritant hair
but which sheds freeways, buses express intentions.
While on the other side everything we do
is read for its entailments in her demanding world.
Considering how much of it reads wagging the dog
how much in the window she is and the derealization
of her regulator tail a two-headed tail.

Coin-cident tail-is-"man" — the lost-in-the-chain,
lowest common denominator charm, say higher
mathematical physics fudge of sweetness and light
between
the heavily fallen bodies.

On January the sixth Jon, when told
said "the epiphany", the day he, immodest editor, died.

After not hearing anything for a few days and then that he'd
had a good week, I dreamt we had just descended
in an elevator in an apartment building vaguely identifiable
but in which I'd never been, on the other side
of Banff Avenue, not far from the cemetery. The doors
opened, the light shone in. Jon gestured into it (he was
a great gesturer) with one hand, and with the other
touched his chest, sweatered, as often, but with a cross.
His face was plumper.

Mid morning Alice phoned to say *that*
he had died.

On the one hand Jon was a literalist and stubborn empiricist.
On the other, compensatingly, he was drawn to the ghost
story, albeit in a mock style.

Perhaps his poem "Paley"
is a common solution.

Jon quoted "like a puma perched upon a pine" in a preface
as an example of his youthful folly, keeping it propelled
just the same, with a small remittance.

This can easily fall into corny psychic technology
but my grandmother saw Uncle Homer's face flash in a dream,
just before they learned
his Lancaster was unaccounted for.

I don't usually remember my dreams,
what did it mean?

There is a reflex in the plane
that implicates one
in another's life, set, free.

In Mr. Steer's now gone, though not the building
nor a business, beside the Paris where Jon really
connote-worthiedy himself, and when I was on direct drive
from Lethbridge Pil to poetry, he was expatiating
on his latest investigations, the word 'turn',
tried to suck all poetry for the rest of the evening
into this word's turns, its etymology turned *on* itself.

Another time beside the Magpie and Stump on a summer's day
(I can hear him with this
gentle cliché interleave [a haunting pun now] his erudition)
Jon respectfully introduced me to a woman
and asked if I'd ever thought about the word 'teem' (no pun)
as in "a teeming brain" he suggested for starters,
then "a teeming salmon". We looked upstream
on such a Bloomsday and hazel bough. Now who looks out
from the interleaf? Davey on Purdy, Purdy on Davey
"Bloomed" with Cameron. Davey on CameronBirney
haunted alike by bloom and blank. His "lack"
haunted by the flesh.

Years before in the winter of '71
Earle "Bird" was in the Whyte Foundation Archives
putting his Earley memories of Banff on tape.
Passing through the doorway
whose door advertized his reading beside a poster of Einstein
he quipped "two local boys" just like: the milkman whipped
he recorded, over his shoulder over the milk cans
to the back of the wagon
where Earle sat with his newspapers very particular
watching the receding town command/obey his expanding,
finishing reflection/alienation, bringing home Bacon's
rolling piggyback observation to a constant aught, big fat
zero for an old world starting out fresh science.

Later Earl*him* and Noble*me* walked by the Magpie and Stump
which was then a Chinese restaurant called the Modern Cafe.
(Jon, index finger hooked over the bridge of his large lenses
to the bridge of his nose, "the White Owl before that".)
We dropped one another on Banff Avenue. Later of course
I could drop him more than he could drop me, breaking our
relativity. (The postal coded TOL OCO Guys was a two-piece
Banff band.) Jon loved to drop and address those given
to ungava, the met-a-world of poets once a parachute always
jumping in.

I told him maybe it was that generation up against
a more quietly more "manly" world — Earle talking about being
a skinny kid and then finally filling out, the number of
chin-ups he could do. Al Purdy telling us how tall and how
heavy he was at sixteen (6' 1" x 180 lbs.) and repeating it
on *Morningside*. Jon thought I was attacking them
and as poets too! Bang, he sicks two heavyweights on me.
Jon, the skinniest, could do Russian dancing, one-legged
squats and hand clapping pushups, between cigarettes.
Only at parties! He beat me at thumb wrestling.

He said I said "weight training" was what I did and so
what was I training for? But I never used that phrase.
Jon the empiricist abstracting me into his joke.
What I said was "I can hardly wait — lift!"

Just now almost three months after his death
and one month after I started this poem (Frye says all
the diachronics flip into a synchrony according to first
the incarnate *verb* and then the verbal
lifting and continuing the *verb*) I was
sitting in one of the many new coffee bars, the one where
the King Eddy used to be, reading the paper when
the proprietor dumped a load of cups and saucers and spoons
into the bus tray just behind my head. I guess my shoulders
were pretty reflexive but also synchronized an instant parody

on the strength of the field-conditioning witnesses. Shoulder
language from behind is certainly not a dead language,
ignorable yes, not official and yet rescuable and sometimes,
o lawful Newton and the Echimamish, skeweringly cue-able.
He let out a loud "Oh, I'm sorry" as if I hadn't conscripted him
and the packed-in clientele broke into an uproar, symphony for
strings
strung out into what's the rest of it. The fall
of the first foot, birth, and rise of modern music.

One of the clients was Brian Patton, buddy of Jon's
who had just gotten back from two months in Arizona
unable to write the book he had a deadline for.
Instead he was compiling an anthology of Jon's columns.
The one he gave to the *Crag* they reprinted after the funeral
from their own known nerve on nerve put out
was the one where Jon had Big Eddy and Little Tommy
jump back into life
trying to recognize the fallen reverb of a place. Little
Tommy says to Big Eddy, "There ain't no Eddy, Eddy"

Footnotes are
upon us, eponymous.